A Warrior Bishop of the Twelfth Century
The *Deeds of Albero* of Trier, by Balderich

Balderich's *Deeds of Albero* offers important insight into the conflicts between church and state during the twelfth century. The *Gesta Alberonis* records the exploits of Albero von Montreuil (Archbishop of Trier, 1131–1152), portrayed as a daring hero doing battle on behalf of the "Liberty of the Church."

During the late eleventh and early twelfth centuries, political and ecclesiastical rulers alike sought to clarify the responsibilities, rights, and obligations they had in common and those that were unique to their different but related kinds of rule. Balderich opens Albero's *Deeds* with explicit reference to these struggles for power, which later came to be known as the Investiture Controversy. This conflict between the church and the German emperor centred on the question of control over the appointment of bishops: clergy and princes alternately allied with and fought against one another, seeking to consolidate their respective powers through different structures of governance.

As a young cleric in Metz, Albero resisted an imperially appointed bishop. His audacious use of disguise while traveling on secret missions for his church shows him to be very much a folk-hero. And once Albero had been appointed archbishop, Balderich characterizes him as the linchpin in the actions of popes and kings. Albero attended important church councils, ensured the election of King Conrad III, and led troops on campaigns in Italy and northern Germany. But it was Albero's rule as a prince-bishop that proved paramount. Albero directed the spiritual affairs of the church in Trier while exercising political rule over the principality, and it is the latter that is Balderich's principal focus and makes the *Deeds* the remarkable document it is.

The translation of the *Deeds*, based on Trier, Stadtbibliothek MS no: 1387/6/8°, with accompanying notes, is prefaced by a wide-ranging historical introduction. The volume includes maps, a selected bibliography, and an index.

MEDIAEVAL SOURCES IN TRANSLATION 44

A Warrior Bishop of the Twelfth Century

The *Deeds of Albero* of Trier,

by Balderich

Translated, with an introduction and notes, by

BRIAN A. PAVLAC

PONTIFICAL INSTITUTE OF MEDIAEVAL STUDIES

LIBRARY AND ARCHIVES CANADA CATALOGUING IN PUBLICATION

Balderich, of Florennes, d. ca. 1157

A warrior bishop of the twelfth century : the Deeds of Albero of Trier / by Balderich ; translated, with an introduction and notes, by Brian A. Pavlac.

(Mediaeval sources in translation, ISSN 0316–0874 ; 44)
Translation of: Gesta Alberonis.
Includes bibliographical references and index.
ISBN 978-0-88844-294-9

1. Albero, von Montreuil, Archbishop of Trier, ca. 1080–1152.
2. Church renewal – Catholic Church – History – To 1500.
3. Church state – History – To 1500.   4. Church history – 12th century.
5. Catholic Church – Germany – Trier Region – Bishops – Biography.
6. Bishops –Germany – Trier Region – Biography.   7. Trier Region (Germany) – Church history.   I. Pavlac, Brian Alexander, 1956–
II. Stadtbibliothek Trier. Manuscript. 1387/6/8°.   III. Title.   IV. Series.

PA8257.B3G4813 2008   282.092   C2008-900670-4

Contents

Preface

When the medieval schoolmaster Balderich wrote a biography to commemorate his friend Albero von Montreuil (Archbishop of Trier from 1131 to 1152), he provided us with an intriguing historical source. Archbishop Albero may not be well-known today, but, as the *The Deeds of Albero* tries to highlight, he played a significant role in the Western Latin Church, the German Empire, and the territories along the Mosel river. Concentrating on the heroic cleric's exploits in all these areas, Balderich's work offers both an entertaining and instructive account of the tumultuous early twelfth century. Church and state were trying to sort out their different but overlapping roles. Albero's weaving together of politics and religion can still speak to us today.

This first translation into English of Albero's biography is based on Trier, Stadtbibliothek MS no. 1387/6/8°. The labours of translation have taken longer but proved more enjoyable than I anticipated. I thank the Stadtbibliothek of Trier for allowing me to use this precious manuscript and its picture of Albero for the cover. Evelyn S. Firchow and Hans Fix made some valuable contributions, as did Fred Unwalla and Jean Hoff of the Pontifical Institute for Mediaeval Studies and the press's anonymous readers.

I dedicate this work to my spouse, Elizabeth Susan Lott. Her reading and her suggestions about both the Latin and my English helped me improve it in many ways; only her constant love and support have enabled me to complete this work.

Introduction

Balderich's *Gesta Alberonis* or the *Deeds of Albero* presents an exciting and revealing record of a remarkable prelate and of the age in which he lived. The portrait drawn of Albero von Montreuil, Archbishop of Trier (r. 1131–1152), that emerges shows him to be an energetic prince-bishop involved in church reform, imperial politics, and territorial rule during the first half of the twelfth century. Albero often worked with Pope Innocent II, Pope Eugene III, and Bernard of Clairvaux to assert the independence of the Church. He clashed with the Emperors Henry V and Lothar III and helped elect King Conrad III to maintain the Church's freedoms. Finally, and perhaps centrally, Albero fought to establish a strong archiepiscopal territorial state in the region of the lower Mosel and middle Rhine in western Germany.

This introduction first examines the author of the *Deeds* against the historical background of the so-called Investiture Controversy. A survey of Albero's roles in the Western Latin Church, in the German Empire, and in the territorial politics of Trier follows, providing the context for Balderich's biography. A brief note on the source and translation of the *Deeds* is appended.

Little is known about the author of the *Deeds of Albero*. Of his early years, Balderich says only that he was born at Florennes in the diocese of Liège. By 1147 Balderich was already an accomplished clerical scholar in Paris and well versed in papal issues when he attracted the attention of Archbishop Albero, who had come there to visit the pope. Impressed with Balderich's disputations Albero invited him to become master of the cathedral school in Trier.

Later, the great Abbot Wibald of Stavelot and Corvey encouraged Balderich's talent and praised his scholarship.[1]
Balderich seems to have outlived his patron Albero by
about ten years; sometime after 1163 he ceases to be mentioned in local records. But for fifteen years Balderich
played an important role in local affairs in Trier. He held
the positions of cathedral schoolmaster and provost of the
collegial foundation St. Simeon (which was housed in the
famous Porta Nigra, an old Roman city gate). Shortly after
Albero's death, Balderich wrote the *Deeds of Albero*, apparently his only literary work.

Balderich's sources for his narrative include his personal knowledge of Albero and conversations with others
who knew the archbishop, written records, and a brief
biography composed in verse by an unknown cleric during
Albero's later years.[2] Balderich's chapters on Albero's youth
are the least reliable. These sections, detailing Albero's near-
legendary youthful exploits, contain several errors of chronology and fact. Lacking first-hand knowledge, Balderich
relies on two documents to fill out his account: an imperial
letter describing the events in Rome in 1111 and a letter to
the pope about the problems with the elections in Trier in
1130. But from the account of Albero's accession onwards,
the *Deeds* is generally trustworthy in the overall picture it
provides, even if chronology tends to be compressed.
Events after Balderich's arrival in Trier in 1147, such as the

1. Wibald of Stavelot, *Epistolae* 91, ed. Philip Jaffé in *Bibliotheca
rerum Germanicarum,* 6 vols. (Berlin, 1864–1873), 1:164–5: "Therefore, praising your industriousness, we ask by your fatherly, but deepest
affection and we urge in the Lord, that you may not allow that noble and
very bright intelligence of yours which was implanted by nature, with
God providing for you, and was cultivated during your youth in the best
possible ways, to languish through inactivity." Stephanie Haarländer,
*Vitae episcoporum: Eine Quellengattung zwischen Hagiographie und
Historiographie, untersucht an Lebensbeschreibungen von Bischöfen
des Regnum Teutonicum im Zeitalter der Ottonen und Salier* (Stuttgart,
2000), pp. 82–5, notes Balderich's unusual self-awareness.
2. The so-called *Gesta Metrica:* see MGH *Scriptores,* 8:236–42.

conflict over castle Treis or the papal visit in 1147–1148, clearly represent eye-witness accounts. Balderich's perspective is often limited to Albero's field of action and usually lacks an overall view of social, political, religious, and economic forces in the Empire. Still, taken as a whole, Balderich's biography accurately recounts the major events of Albero's life and reign.

The *Deeds*, however, does not offer an objective portrait of Albero. Balderich clearly wrote the work to honor an exemplary prince-bishop, casting Albero as a major hero who rises to greatness and whose actions shape his times. As such, it corresponds more to the *gesta* (deeds) devoted to historical figures than to the episcopal *vitae* (lives) composed by other contemporary writers:[3] the work is biography, and bears little resemblance to hagiography or to saints' lives. Albero performs no religious wonders or miracles. Indeed, in comparison with other biographies of bishops, or episcopal *vitae*, the *Deeds* lacks many details concerning Albero's religious duties or his own individual spirituality.[4] Only the description of his performance of the mass and his deathbed confession of faith at the end of the work belatedly reveal a personal piety. Balderich passes over even typical episcopal duties (such as dedicating

3. See Oskar Köhler, *Das Bild des geistlichen Fürsten in den Viten des 10., 11. und 12. Jahrhunderts* (Berlin, 1935), esp. pp. 127–8, 131–2, 138, for Albero. Jörg R. Müller, *Vir religiosus ac strenuus: Albero von Montreuil, Erzbischof von Trier, 1132–1152* (Trier, 2006), pp. 743–4, sees *The Deeds* as the first biography of its kind of a *Reichsbischof*.
4. See Stephanie Coué, *Hagiographie im Kontext: Schreibanlass und Funktion von Bischofsviten aus dem 11. and vom Anfang des 12. Jahrhunderts* (Berlin and New York, 1997), who argues that writers of earlier espiscopal *vitae* had several goals: seeking to assert the claims or prestige of a church, providing a warning to successors, or defending a bishop's character; see also C. Stephen Jaeger, *The Origins of Courtliness: Civilizing Trends and the Formation of Courtly Ideals, 939–1210* (Philadelphia, 1985), esp. pp. 28–40, for examples of specific virtues applied to courtier-clerics in contemporary *vitæ*. Haarländer, *Vitae episcoporum*, pp. 171–3, 297–304, compares Balderich's version with those of other contemporaries.

churches, appointing priests, supervising religious life, visiting parishes). The few descriptions of Albero's character and person which Balderich includes, such as his slowness, his love of intellectual conversation, or the challenges posed to his preaching by both a poor grasp of German and an attempt to convey profound ideas, emerge only toward the end of the text. Balderich also does not align Albero's actions with those of the expanding papacy. Albero respects the popes, but also tries to gain from them privileges and offices to further his own objectives in Lotharingia. The phenomenon of prince-bishops evolved from the weak governments of the early Middle Ages. Since the fall of the Roman Empire, bishops held high status as literate leaders of Christian communities. The "barbarian" kings, who had replaced the Roman emperors, senators, and consuls, often worked with the bishops to maintain what governance they could. For their part, many bishops either seized power that had been lost by imperial administrators or received authority with royal consent. Such bishops continued to perform their spiritual duties of baptism, preaching, and consecration, while pursuing the more worldly tasks of supervising agricultural estates, collecting revenues, advising princes, holding court, and even building up military power.

Entering the High Middle Ages, the kings of the Ottonian Dynasty (919–1024) and the successor Salian Dynasty (1024–1125) had transformed the German Empire, which later became the Holy Roman Empire, into the most powerful state in Europe. This state consisted of four kingdoms: the German (covering today's Germany, the Netherlands, Luxembourg, Alsace and Lorraine of France, Switzerland, and Austria), Burgundian (France east of the Rhône), Lombard (Northern Italy), and Bohemian (the Czech Republic) kingdoms. The German Kingdom dominated the others, as it did Europe, until the twelfth century. The ruler of the German Kingdom usually called himself

King of the Romans, as if continuing the Roman Empire of antiquity, and within a few years of his royal coronation, the pope would crown him Emperor of the Romans (later called Holy Roman Emperor).

During this consolidation of power, the leading German prelates and the German kings strengthened their mutually beneficial political and economic arrangements.[5] In return for the donation of royal possessions and associated political jurisdiction (known as *regalia*) to the German church, the German kings substantially controlled the selection of higher clergy and their subsequent investiture, or installation, into office. Thus the prince-bishops acquired land and power, while the king hoped to secure administrators and allies who would prove more reliable than hereditary nobles. (The kings of England and France promoted similar cooperation with their bishops, though they succeeded to a lesser degree.)

The Investiture Controversy of 1076–1122 threatened these arrangements.[6] This quarrel, largely between the popes of the Roman Church and the kings of the German Empire over the divisions of secular and spiritual jurisdiction, colored the views of the next generation, including those of Balderich. While it also affected England and France, it transformed the German Empire. The Investiture

5. This arrangement has been sometimes called the Ottonian–Salian imperial church system (*Das ottonisch-salische Reichskirchensystem*). The relationships between king and bishops were not so much systematically or legally regulated but rather were based on circumstance, personality, and local customs. Timothy Reuter, "The 'Imperial Church System' of the Ottonian and Salian Rulers: A Reconsideration," *Journal of Ecclesiastical History* 33 (1982): 347–74, criticizes this scholarly construct, while Josef Fleckenstein, "Problematik und Gestalt der ottonisch-salischen Reichskirche," in *Reich und Kirche vor dem Investiturstreit: Vorträge beim wissenschaftlichen Kolloquium aus Anlaß des achtzigsten Geburtstags von Gerd Tellenbach*, ed. Karl Schmid (Sigmaringen, 1985), pp. 83–98, offers a defense.

6. Uta-Renate Blumenthal, *The Investiture Controversy: Church and Monarchy from the Ninth to the Twelfth Century* (Philadelphia, 1988), provides an excellent overview.

Controversy originated with those clerics in the Western Latin Church who began to reform the papacy during the mid-eleventh century. By the late eleventh century, reformers had elevated the pope, nominally the Bishop of Rome, into the spiritual and administrative head of the Christian hierarchy in Western Europe. Sometimes known as the Gregorian or Hildebrandine Reform, after one of the leading promoters of reform, Hildebrand, who later became Pope Gregory VII (r. 1073–1085), this movement drew on the efforts of many reforming clerics throughout Christendom who aimed to discipline and purify the church through an expansion of papal control, the enforcement of clerical celibacy, and the elimination of the purchase of church offices (a practice called simony).

The clerical reformers soon sought to limit any involvement by secular rulers in Church affairs, especially in the appointment of bishops. They claimed, correctly, that canon (or Church) law required bishops to be chosen by the people of the diocese, not kings. They also specifically attacked the overt act of investiture, whereby the German king handed a bishop his symbols of spiritual office, the ring (representing his marriage to the church) and staff (showing his authority to guide his flock). The reformers feared corruption of spiritual matters by the political and material interests of powerful laymen.[7] The motto of the reform movement, "*Libertas æcclesiæ*" or "Liberty of the Church," reflects this ideal.

Balderich's use of the term three times (in Chapters 2, 8, and 16) shows how the ideology of the Investiture Controversy came to dominate his perspective. He begins by setting Albero's life in the context of this conflict between popes and emperors, although the account he offers is mistaken, opening as it does with the right pope, but, in Henry III, with the wrong emperor. Ironically, it

---

7. See Susan Wood, *The Proprietary Church in the Medieval West* (Oxford, 2006), p. 856.

was Emperor Henry III (r. 1039–1056) who essentially established the reform movement by appointing several reforming popes in Rome. Under Henry III's son, King (later Emperor) Henry IV (r. 1056–1106), open conflict broke out with Pope Gregory VII. Civil wars ravaged the German Empire through two generations as kings, papal reformers, church prelates, and magnates in Germany and the cities in Lombardy took sides, depending on their own interests.

At the heart of the conflict was the position of prince-bishops. The letter cited by Balderich in Chapters 3–6 of the *Deeds* underlines the issue. It dates to the time when Henry V (r. 1106–1125) sought to have himself crowned emperor in 1111 by Pope Paschal II (r. 1099–1118). Radical reformers resented the son as much as they had the father, Henry IV, and insisted on his renouncing investiture before any coronation. Henry V, in turn, was willing to give up his rights over bishops, provided they no longer held political power. If this extraordinary compromise had succeeded, prince-bishops would have ceased to exist, and bishops would have, as they do today, restricted themselves to Church affairs. The aristocratic German prelates, however, could not accept the loss of their secular authority.

So the conflict dragged on until 1122, with the compromise of the Concordat of Worms between Pope Calixtus II (r. 1119–1124) and Emperor Henry V. That treaty allowed the German king some influence over the higher clergy in three distinct ways. First, the monarch could be present during local ecclesiastical elections by clergy and could mediate disputed elections. Next, the monarch could invest the candidate with the *regalia* by means of a symbol of temporal power, such as a staff or flag, thus preserving the royal connection with the candidate. Finally, the bishops of the church could consecrate the bishop-elect, thereby asserting the spiritual authority of the clergy. The description of Albero's election in the *Deeds* shows the influence of this compromise and its continuing complications.[8] Overall, the Investiture Controversy transformed the entire structure of government and society in the German Empire, shaping the views of Albero's generation and determining Albero's own policies.

The consequences were significant. First, the warfare between kings, dukes, and bishops promoted the use of the ministerials, or servile knights.[9] Like serfs, who were bound to the lord's land, ministerials were also legally unfree persons; however, they differed from serfs in being bound by service to a lord and in having the right to bear arms. Originally, feudal lords had created the class of ministerials, or serf-knights, to aid them in both combat and governance, since their legal subservience made them more reliable than feudal vassals. But during times of crisis, ministerials slowly lost their servile position because their lords made concessions to retain their loyalty. Paid and rewarded with lands and jurisdictions, they became powerful in their own right and sought to rival the lay nobility in status. Albero's conflict with the local ministerials led by Ludwig de Ponte (see below) demonstrates this trend, and is described in one of the most interesting passages of the *Deeds*.

Second, the decline in centralized power that occurred after Henry V and before the reign of Emperor Frederick Barbarossa (r. 1152–1190) encouraged the local nobility and aristocrats to expand their own power and authority. During these years, many imperial magnates and princes, both lay and clerical, began to build up their local rule and dominion. The resulting power complexes would eventually become the near-sovereign territorial principalities (kingdoms, electorates, duchies, counties, etc.) of the Holy Roman Empire. As a prince-bishop, Albero defended his

8. See Robert L. Benson, *The Bishop-Elect: A Study in Medieval Ecclesiastical Office* (Princeton, 1968), esp. p. 271.

9. Benjamin Arnold, *German Knighthood, 1050–1300* (Oxford, 1985) and John B. Freed, "Reflections on the Medieval German Nobility," *The American Historical Review* 91 (1986): 553–75.

ecclesiastical properties, gained through generations of royal gifts and autonomous acquisitions, and sought to expand both his secular and spiritual jurisdiction and authority. Albero's battles with the Count of Luxemburg and the Counts Palatine reflect this development of local power.

Third, prince-bishops retained much of their political power, worldly wealth, and military might and could shift the balance of power within the German Empire. With less royal control over clerical offices, the German kings had to incorporate the higher clergy into the feudal political system in order to ensure some loyalty and dependence. Since prince-bishops functioned both as church prelates and as feudal rulers, they wielded both spiritual and temporal swords in their territories. As a result, they often had to apportion their loyalty: to their cathedral church and its temporalities, to the king, or to their own family or local interests.

The opening chapter of the *Deeds* sets the tone for Albero's unique role in this milieu. Balderich declares that, even without the advantage of great inherited power and on the smaller stage of the territory or kingdom, Albero's achievements still surpass those of the great conquering heroes of the past. These achievements, however, depend neither on lineage nor great wealth. Albero's family background had little bearing on his success.[10] It was his actions that brought him honor and renown. Balderich shows that a man need possess only a native intelligence and an unshakeable faith to succeed: Albero triumphs and even influences the course of historical events through his ingenuity, his personal charisma, and his great heroic spirit.

10. Only after relating Albero's youthful adventures does Balderich mention that Albero's parents were noble and from the Toul bishopric. On his family, the petty nobles of Thicourt-Montreuil and their connections, see Michel Parisse, *Noblesse et chevalerie en Lorraine médiévale: Les familles nobles du XIe au XIIIe siècle* (Nancy, 1982), pp. 133–6, and Müller, *Vir religiosus ac strenuous*, pp. 43–80.

In the second chapter, Balderich compares Albero to Alexander and Charlemagne, declaring him a heroic defender of the Holy Church. Moreover, he fulfils this purpose by using the instruments of this world, not the next: the *Deeds* portrays a hero who enjoys and even glories in his princely power and authority, both secular and spiritual, and who deploys the force of words no less than of arms to increase the prosperity of the Church, whether in Metz or Trier. Balderich's portrait is not without its exaggerations or improbabilities. Albero is central to nearly every event described in the *Deeds*: saints, popes, kings, and magnates all play a supporting role, reacting to Albero's active engagement with history. In reality, Albero was only one player among many and, in matters outside his archbishopric in Trier, seldom the most important. It is Balderich's heroic vision that makes Albero the pivotal figure he becomes in the *Deeds*.

Albero's early, rather fantastic exploits in his home diocese of Metz are especially illustrative of the heroic cast Balderich gives to his subject. These youthful adventures, which take place during the Investiture Controversy, center on Albero's efforts to replace Bishop Adalberon (1090–1121), who had sided with the emperor against a reform-minded candidate. The tone of the description also serves to heighten the entire later history. Balderich intended the escapades to be believed, since he directly qualifies only one of them.[11] Other contemporary sources confirm the description of Albero's opposition to the imperial bishop in Metz, the emperor's hostility toward Albero, and Albero's

11. In the episode in Chapter 10 describing Albero spying on Henry V and obtaining alms from his wife, Empress Mathilda, Balderich uses the phrases "it is said" and "it is added," perhaps to indicate hearsay or second-hand information. Marjorie Chibnall does not include the story in her account of Mathilda's German experience in *The Empress Mathilda: Queen Consort, Queen Mother and Lady of the English* (Oxford, 1991), pp. 18–50. A similar incident, however, is also found in the *Gesta Metrica*, MGH *Scriptores* 8:237.30–40. Note also Balderich's opening prologue, Chapter 1, claiming the truthfulness of his work.

use of disguise.[12] But within the various escapades, it is impossible to determine with certainty which details are historically genuine and which the invention of popular tradition. Some of the exploits, especially those describing Albero's disguises, clearly draw on common folkloric themes.[13] Balderich's emphasis on Albero's simple origins links them to the world of the fairy tale, in which the lowly protagonist confounds the rich and powerful through his fortitude, cleverness, and deeds. His disguises, as servant, beggar, merchant, or cripple, are echoed in episodes from courtly epics such as *König Rother* or *Salman und Morolf,* which would appear within the next few decades, providing further evidence of the intermingling of history and legend after Albero's lifetime.

How is a modern reader to understand these adventures? These tales, and the larger history of which they are part, did not merely provide a factual account of Albero's life. Instead, Balderich aims to teach by example, to show the clerical readers that constitute the main audience of the book how God could work in this world through one of their own.[14] The *Deeds* aspires to provide its contemporary readers with a model of a twelfth-century clerical hero. Specifically, Albero's career is intended to inspire secular clerics committed to the spiritual church, but involved in temporal affairs. The emphasis on cleverness and on bold action must have had a great appeal to a clergy who ran the

12. See especially the *Vita Theogeri,* ed. Philip Jaffé, MGH *Scriptores,* 12:449–79, written in the Lotharingian cloister of Prüfening, ca. 1138–1146.

13. Friedrich Panzer, "Erzbischof Albero von Trier und die Deutschen Spielmannsepen," in *Germanistische Abhandlungen, Hermann Paul zum 17. März 1902 dargebracht* (Strasbourg, 1902), pp. 303–32.

14. See Alfred Ebenbauer, "Das Dilemma der Wahrheit: Gedanken zum 'historisierenden Roman' des 13. Jahrhunderts," *Geschichtsbewußtsein in der deutschen Literatur des Mittelalters: Tübinger Colloquium 1983* (Tübingen, 1985), pp. 59, 68; and Johannes Spörl, *Grundformen hochmittelalterliche Geschichtsanschauung: Studien zur Weltbild der Geschichtsschreiber des 12. Jahrhunderts* (Darmstadt, 1968), especially p. 20.

bureaucracy and administration of an expanding territorial principality, for it demonstrated that intelligence, education, and resolve, not the sanctity of person or office, might serve to elevate their social and political position and that of their church.

By Chapter 15, the focus shifts from the conflict over the episcopacy of Metz to the political expansion of the new archbishop of Trier. Key to Albero's success was his close relation to popes, prelates, and other ecclesiastical officials of the period. His determined efforts to place a reforming bishop in the cathedral of Metz had established his fame among reformers and brought him infamy among the imperial party. While Balderich exaggerates the attempts to elect Albero to the see of Halberstadt and the see of Magdeburg, both located in Saxony far from his native Lotharingia, Albero's involvement in these elections attests to a reputation for good counsel and to a reforming spirit. Moreover, he befriended two men later canonized as saints. First, Albero played a role in the election of Norbert of Xanten, founder of the Premonstratentian Order, as Archbishop of Magdeburg. Albero also found a friend and supporter in perhaps the greatest religious figure of the age, Bernard of Clairvaux (d. 1153), who so dominates the second quarter of the twelfth century that it is often called the "Age of Saint Bernard." Bernard supported Albero's subjugation of the monastery of St. Maximin, mediated the resulting dispute with the Count of Luxemburg, and visited Trier several times.[15] Balderich's singleminded focus on Albero leaves no room for the Abbot of Clairvaux, who is not mentioned in the *Gesta*.[16]

---

15. Bernard's concrete support came in the form of several letters to the pope: see *The Letters of St. Bernard of Clairvaux*, trans. Bruno Scott James (Kalamazoo, 1998), nos. 218–22.

16. Albero, on the other hand, does not rate mention in Adriaan H. Bredero, *Bernard of Clairvaux: Between Cult and History* (Grand Rapids, MI, 1996).

The most important clerical support Albero possessed was that of the papacy. Albero's early adventures show his close contact with the Roman curia. Papal pressure overcame his reluctance to accept his election as archbishop of the troubled see of Trier, where he lacked family connections or any personal power base. Once consecrated as archbishop in 1131, Albero's ecclesiastical policy reflects both his close relations to the papacy and increasing papal involvement in local matters. Far more than his predecessors, Albero received papal charters confirming the privileges of his see and his own great authority. Pope Innocent II (r. 1130–1143) made Albero the papal legate for Germany in 1137 as a special mark of favor. The position of the pope's official representative normally went to the more prestigious sees of Mainz or Cologne, but the see of Mainz was vacant and the archbishop-elect of Cologne was as yet unconsecrated. Albero gained the legateship probably because, with the approaching death of Emperor Lothar (d. 1137), the papal curia saw the need for a strong hand in Germany (see below). Albero's acquisition of the honor briefly boosted the power and prestige of Trier against his rival Rhenish archbishops and ensured him a significant role mediating between the papacy and the German royal court at the time of King Conrad's election in 1138.[17] A rare papal visit to Trier over Christmas 1147 by Pope Eugene III (r. 1145–1153) further reflects papal support for Albero.[18]

Of course, papal support was not always forthcoming. The pope refused to back Albero's ambitious effort to increase the prestige of his church (and himself) by elevating Trier to supremacy within the old Roman province of Belgic

17. Müller, *Vir religiosus ac strenuous*, pp. 553, 686–96, observes that Albero's military and territorial interests distracted him from developing the legateship, but also helped him take charge of Conrad's election.

18. Helmut Gleber, *Papst Eugen III. (1145–1153) unter besonderer Berücksichtigung seiner politischen Tätigkeit* (Jena, 1936), pp. 80–2, notes Eugene's attempt to gain support in Germany.

Gaul and over the most important French see, Rheims. Still, Albero's very attempt in making the claim, and the apology he secured from the archbishop of Rheims over the resulting brawl (Chapter 29), is evidence of his power and the esteem in which he was held. Albero's aspirations extended not only to honor and authority over a broad swath of Europe but also to closer supervision of monasteries and churches in his own diocese. In the twelfth century, bishops commonly subjected local spiritual institutions to diocesan control. Albero's ostensible goal of monastic reform, a dose of discipline or regeneration for lax monastic life, in this case even received the support of Bernard of Clairvaux before the Roman curia. Although ignored by Balderich, Albero's foundation of new cloisters at Himmerod and Springiersbach, for example, extended archiepiscopal authority, promoted a disciplined clergy, developed new land, and provided new revenues.[19] His attempts to dominate established institutions such as St. Florin in Coblenz and St. Maximin, however, were frustrated by legal appeals to the papal curia in Rome. Both sides produced forgeries to bolster their claims, but the curia initially favored St. Maximin's.

Although closely bound to leaders of the church, Albero also dealt with rulers of the German Empire. While still a cleric in Metz, Albero had been outlawed by King Henry V. His early opposition to this king is clear, even if the amusing tales of his spying on and taunting of the king may be exaggerations. No sooner had the Investiture Controversy been resolved, however, than a new crisis faced the German Empire. Henry V died in 1125 leaving no male heir. The leading German magnates and high clergy first elected Lothar von Supplinburg from Saxony (r. 1125–1137), followed by Conrad von Staufen from Swabia (r. 1138–1152). Each came from different dynasties and regions, and each faced resistance to his claim to the throne.

19. Müller, *Vir religiosus ac strenuous*, pp. 227–354, working from the documents, gives priority to Albero's efforts in this area.

Albero's initial relations with King Lothar III von Supplinburg were strained and did not substantially improve
anytime later. The archiepiscopal election in Trier had
posed difficulties for Lothar, who had been unable to mediate the dispute. Albero's election by a small contingent
and his consecration by the pope before his royal investiture with the *regalia*, in direct violation of the Concordat
of Worms, only complicated matters. Albero's oath of
respect toward royal prerogatives helped Lothar save face,
and he later invested Albero with the *regalia*. Albero then
asserted his loyalty to Church reform and his own territorial interests by excommunicating Lothar's brother, the
Duke of Upper Lotharingia, for encroaching on the prerogatives of church in Toul, although the latter soon
repented. One modern historian claims Albero was Lothar's
chief nemesis among the prelates, but this seems an exag-
geration.[20] Still, Albero rarely attended Lothar's court and
in 1136 apparently only accompanied Lothar's second Italian expedition (with fewer knights than expected) mainly
in order to wheedle the monastery of St. Maximin out of
the king.

Perhaps even more fraught than his relationship with
the king were those within Trier itself. Balderich tellingly
describes the troubled state of Trier, from the death in
prison of Albero's immediate predecessor to the seizure of
the temporal administration by the ministerials (which
may account for Albero's reluctance to accept the post).

20. Marie-Louise Crone, *Untersuchungen zur Reichskirchenpolitik
Lothars III. (1125–1127) zwischen reichskirchlicher Tradition und Re-
formkurie* (Frankfurt am Main, 1982), pp. 94–7, 248, comments that
Albero gave "the death blow to Lothar's life work." With more modera-
tion, Wolfgang Petke, *Kanzlei, Kapelle und königliche Kurie unter Lothar
III (1125–1137)* (Cologne and Vienna, 1985), pp. 254–7, concludes from
Albero's rare visits to Lothar's court and from events surrounding his
election that relations between Lothar and Albero were, not surprisingly,
rather cool. Wolfram Ziegler, "Studien zur staufischen Opposition unter
Lothar III. (1125–1137)," *Concilium medii aevi* 10 (2007): 79–83, con-
cedes to Albero merely a distant relationship with Lothar.

The leader of the ministerials, Ludwig de Ponte, had slowly risen in power until as the burgrave or prefect of the city he held authority as Trier's military commander. In a remarkable passage in the *Deeds* (Chapter 17), Ludwig argues for a position diametrically opposed to that of the Gregorian reformers: if laymen have no place in the Church's spiritual business, then churchmen should have no role in secular affairs, he claims. In effect, Ludwig sought to reduce the archbishop to a spiritual shepherd, while arrogating to himself temporal lordship over vast archiepiscopal possessions. Without control over revenues, the political power of the archbishops of Trier would have dissipated. Albero successfully brought Ludwig to terms, without violence.[21] Despite his triumph in Trier, Albero repeatedly had to juggle his obligations to the pope, to the king, and to the lands and people of his diocese.

The conflict over St. Maximin best illustrates the problems of territorial rule by prince-bishops that dominate the *Deeds*. His success against Ludwig encouraged Albero to expand his dominion still further at the expense of the royal monastery of St. Maximin. At the beginning of Albero's reign, Trier's temporalities were scattered throughout the Mosel region, but concentrated in two main areas. The much larger upper foundation centered on Trier and the lower Saar; a smaller lower foundation was based at Coblenz and Humbach. The archbishop was determined to secure the integrity of both regions and connect them along the land route over Wittlich and Mayen or along the Mosel River. As the last independent spiritual institution near Trier — it sat right outside the city gates — St. Maximin and its vast possessions along the Mosel and Saar and in the Eifel greatly tempted the archbishop. Since the discipline of its monks was admirable, Albero's key motive for

---

21. While the *Deeds* often focus on Albero's bold actions, Müller, *Vir religiosus ac strenuus* pp. 217–8, 751, notes how this conflict well illustrates Albero's skill at negotiation and compromise.

bringing St. Maximin under archiepiscopal control certainly rested on the proprietary and judicial rights of that foundation. If Albero could nominate the abbot, the archbishop's court would become the ordinary court for all monastic judicial disputes, and episcopal officials would supervise the monastery's scattered temporalities.

Although both pope and king had initially turned Albero down, a change came with Lothar's successor, King Conrad III von Staufen in whose election Albero had played the key role.[22] This was only natural since Albero was not only the leading prelate in Germany upon Lothar's death but also now papal legate. Conrad, in turn, richly rewarded Albero with the Abbey of St. Maximin in 1139. This time, Albero's forgeries were favored over St. Maximin's.

Unfortunately for Albero's plans, the abbey's advocates, the Counts of Luxemburg, had also hoped to exploit St. Maximin to increase their own holdings and authority.[23] Advocates were lay nobles originally entrusted with jurisdiction over church property and the dependents thereof and with the aim both of reducing the secular obligations of the clergy and protecting their independence. But increasingly during the twelfth century, advocates expanded their own rule by absorbing these church lands and people into their own noble patrimonies. The Counts of Luxemburg were trying to extend their rule from Echternach toward the Lieser and Kyll rivers. If successful, they would have encircled the archbishop's position at Trier. The young and rash Count Henry IV of Luxemburg (r. 1136–1196) became even more powerful and ambitious after he

22. Müller, ibid., pp. 525–37, 753, explains how Albero did not carry out an insurrection, as is sometimes maintained, but carefully and legally built a network of supporters for Conrad's election.

23. On the Counts of Luxemburg, see John A. Gade, *Luxemburg in the Middle Ages* (Leiden, 1951); on the conflict in general, see Heinrich Büttner, "Der Übergang der Abtei St. Maximin an das Erzstift Trier unter Erzbischof Albero von Montreuil," *Geschichtliche Landeskunde* 5 (1968): 65–77.

inherited the wealthy county of Namur to the north, hence his title the Count of Namur in Balderich's account. Henry was all too willing to defy his feudal lord and weaken his territorial rival, the Archbishop of Trier. The monks of St. Maximin, who resisted their subjugation to Trier, provided Count Henry the opportunity.

The conflict over St. Maximin represents the climax of Balderich's *Deeds of Albero*. In the warfare that resulted between the Archbishop of Trier and the Count of Luxemburg and Namur, Conrad was neither willing nor able to help either Albero or Henry. The ensuing campaigns devastated the region for seven years. The legal basis and means of warfare were according to the *Fehde*. When a free man (or corporation) considered himself wronged by another but was unable to gain justice in the courts, he then sought justice on his own through violence against his enemy, particularly by plundering, burning, and destroying his enemy's lands and wealth, while avoiding direct combat between armies. Only the pressure of Conrad's preparations for the ill-starred Second Crusade (1147–1149) and the weariness of the combatants brought a peace favorable to Albero. In the end, Albero's victorious subjection of St. Maximin assured Trier's dominance in the Eifel, while the Count of Luxemburg's penetration in the area was held to the Kyll river.

Other noble rivals, the Counts Palatine by the Rhine, also contested with Albero for dominion in the Mosel region. By the early twelfth century, the Counts were seeking to expand their authority to the east of Trier along the lower Mosel, across the Hunsrück range of hills, and in the Nahe river valley. Their control of strategic royal castles on the lower Mosel (such as Treis), their dynastic advocacy of wealthy expanding foundations (such as Springiersbach and Maria Laach) and of several foundations in Coblenz and their advocacy of Trier itself granted the Counts Palatine many advantages.[24]

24. On the Counts Palatine see Ruth Gerstner, *Die Geschichte der lothringischen und rheinischen Pfalzgrafschafn von ihrer Anfängen bis zur Ausbildung des Kurterritoriums Pfalz* (Bonn, 1941).

The first Count Palatine to trouble Albero was Otto von Rheineck, who was Count Palatine in the name of his stepson as well as an in-law of King Lothar III. Otto's plot to have the two brothers von Nantersburg seize the archiepiscopal castle of Arras was intended to eliminate an archiepiscopal enclave in an area of Palatinate influence. Albero's successful counterattack confirmed for Balderich and his audience the rightness of Albero's cause.

A conflict over control of the Palatinate allowed Albero to expand further along the lower Mosel. After the death of Otto von Rheineck's stepson, King Conrad ignored Otto's claims and reasserted the title of Count Palatine as an appointed imperial office, eventually conferring it on Herman von Stahleck (r. 1142–1156). By virtue of that office, Herman also became high advocate of Trier and swore fealty to Albero. Herman then vigorously reclaimed the possessions of the Palatinate from the presumptive Otto von Rheineck, while at the same time seeking to extend his own power base along the lower Mosel and Middle Rhine. Outmatched by Herman, Otto slowly lost his earlier possessions and titles.

By late 1148, Otto offered the castle Treis, which had been occupied and fortified by Herman's forces, to his old adversary Archbishop Albero. If Albero took the castle, Otto hoped then to be enfeoffed with it. Albero eagerly accepted the offer of this strategic point on the lower Mosel, which sat in the midst of rich Palatine lands, and kept it in his own power. When Albero successfully defended his exclusive possession of castle Treis, the unforeseen long-term result was that the Counts Palatine ceased to strengthen their power on the lower Mosel and concentrated their interests in the south, towards Mainz and Worms. It was a sign of the changing times that the king's former ecclesiastical partners, the prince-bishops, could weaken his named representative, the Palatine Count. The temporal power granted by the kings to the archbishops over the centuries had led to the accumulation of greater power at the expense of the secular princes.

An incident during the siege of Treis further illustrates the unique power of prince-bishops. In Albero's oration before an expected battle with Count Palatine Herman, he promises his troops entrance to heaven if they fell in combat, as if they were on a crusade.[25] Archbishop Albero here successfully unites the divine power of his spiritual office with the secular goal of defending castles. The occupation of a castle whose ultimate ownership was questionable, and which had not been preceded by the destructive pillaging raids of a *Fehde*, hardly seems deserving of salvation.[26] Operating within the temporal sphere and its jurisdictions, Albero nevertheless brings his spiritual authority to bear on the worldly order, binding the divine and the secular together. The episode illustrates the unique advantages afforded the ecclesiastical prince who chose to combine the spiritual and temporal swords.

Balderich ends the *Deeds* with Albero's deathbed confession, a description of his will and funeral, and a prayer and memorial verses to the fallen hero. Albero died on 18 January 1152, followed less than a month later by King Conrad III. The generation that had witnessed the worst confrontations of the Investiture Controversy was also passing with them. These struggles had weakened German kingship since the death of Emperor Henry III, even as they liberated the clergy from both lay interference and also reliance on secular aid. The increasingly assertive dynastic regional nobility, sometimes allied with the more independent ministerialage, had made potent rivals for the archbishops in the temporal sphere.

25. John R.E. Bliese, "Rhetoric and Morale: A Study of Battle Orations from the Central Middle Ages," *Journal of Medieval History* 15 (1989): 201–26.
26. See Norman Housley, "Crusades Against Christians: Their Origins and Early Development, c. 1000–1216," in *Crusade and Settlement: Papers Read at the First Conference of the Society for the Study of the Crusades and the Latin East and Presented to R.C. Smail* (Cardiff, 1985), pp. 22–4, for Albero and contemporary examples.

Through his determined exploitation of his resources, the force of his own character, and firm use of military might, Albero reinvigorated archiepiscopal temporal rule in Trier against the local nobles and ministerials. In addition to recovering and augmenting the material possessions of the see, Albero ruthlessly checked the encroachments of the Counts Palatine and the Count of Luxemburg. From the leaders of the church he gained privileges and support to secure his authority along the Mosel. He stood steadfast against monarchs who sought to diminish the liberties of the church and placed an ally upon the royal throne. Balderich's description of Albero's adventures and exploits provides a colorful and instructive historical source for the achievements of this heroic prince-bishop.

Note on Sources and Translation

Unfortunately for the fame of both Balderich and Albero, the *Deeds of Albero* has remained obscure, not widely known in the Middle Ages or during our own time. Copies of the work survived only in Trier. This translation is based on the oldest text, preserved in a twelfth-century manuscript in the Stadtbibliothek of Trier, no. 1387/6/8°.[27] This manuscript is clearly closest in time to the author and his subject. The text is written in a clear twelfth-century minuscule from the Trier area, perhaps in Balderich's own hand.[28] It opens with a full-page illustration of Albero himself in vibrant colors and with delicate shading. The only

---

27. See Adolf Becker, *Die deutschen Handschriften der Stadtbibliothek zu Trier*, Beschreibendes Verzeichnis der Handschriften der Stadtbibliothek zu Trier, Heft 7. (Trier, 1911), pp. 48–9; Wilhelm Wattenbach and Franz-Josef Schmale, *Deutschlands Geschichtsquellen im Mittelalter: vom Tode Kaiser Heinrichs V. bis zum Ende des Interregnum* (Darmstadt, 1976), p. 349; Max Manitius, *Geschichte der lateinischen Literatur* (Munich, 1911–31), 3:695; and Haarländer, *Vitae episcoporum*, pp. 481–2.

28. Becker, *Die deutschen Handschriften der Stadtbibliothek zu Trier*, p. 48.

other decorations in the manuscript are the large red
initials that mark chapter-openings, and the final memorial verses, also in red ink. In the fifteenth century, the
Deeds of Albero was bound together with various religious
and mystical works of the fourteenth and fifteenth centuries. Another manuscript of the *Deeds* survives in a fif-
teenth-century copy in Trier. Earlier writers adapted, and
lightly edited, the *Deeds* for the *Gesta Treverorum* (*The
Deeds of the People of Trier*), the history of the archbishops of Trier written periodically up to the eighteenth
century. I have drawn on the modern critical edition by
Waitz in the *Monumenta Germaniae Historica* in correct-
ing obvious orthographical errors in the manuscript or for
the alternate readings it provides from other versions of
the text, but retained the manuscript's chapter divisions.[29]
I have also consulted the translations into German made
by Emil Zenz and Hatto Kallfelz.[30]

In translating the *Deeds* into modern English, I have
tried to bear in mind the needs of a contemporary reader
while nevertheless maintaining the flavor of Balderich's
Latin. For clarity, I have sometimes added a word or phrase,
or paraphrased what a literal rendering would have made
cumbersome. Translations from the Bible are based on the
Revised Standard Version, I have preferred it over King
James or Douay because of its more contemporary prose.
Psalms are numbered according to the Revised Standard
Version. Balderich's few references to authors such as
Horace and Ovid attest to his familiarity with classical
Latin typical for his educated contemporaries. Translations
from classical authors are mine. Throughout, the style of

29. See *Gesta Alberonis archiepiscopi auctore Balderico*, ed. G.
Waitz, MGH *Scriptores* 8:234–60.

30. Emil Zenz, ed. and trans. *Von Erzbischof Gottfried (1124) bis zum
Tode Alberos (1152), Die Taten der Trierer/Gesta Treverorum*, vol. 2.
(Trier, 1958), pp. 29–76, and Hatto Kallfelz, trans., "Taten Erzbischof Al-
beros von Trier, verfaßt von Balderich," *Lebensbeschreibungen einiger
Bischöfe des 10.-12. Jahrhunderts* (Darmstadt, 1973), pp. 543–617.

the *Deeds* is readable, fluent, and unpretentious. Only in those passages in which Balderich affects eloquence or erudition (such as when he elaborately addresses the reader, subjects Albero to fulsome praise, or insists on his piety) does his Latin become prolix and pompous.[31] These occasions are, for the modern reader, mercifully rare. Instead, the greater part of the work is a straightforward description of tumultuous events in a notable life.

31. See, for example, his introduction to the war over St. Maximin, Chapter 21.

The *Deeds of Albero*,
Archbishop of Trier,
by Balderich

[Prologue]

1. As I set out to relate the memorable words and deeds of Archbishop Albero of Trier, I undertake a task which will seem to later readers more miraculous than believable. But in this undertaking, know, reader, that I aim at neither praise nor blame, but only the truth.

[The Investiture Controversy, 1075–1111]

2. We marvel that certain men have done great things, even though such deeds were accomplished with the approval, help, and cooperation of many others; princes of nations, for example, who, as heirs and successors in their fathers' realms, extended their empires with armies made up of subject peoples. Such is the case of Alexander, Julius Caesar and Augustus, Charlemagne, and many others who by their deeds provided rich material for the historians of antiquity.[1]

Albero, however, deserves special admiration because he accomplished great deeds by himself, as a private citizen, indeed even while still a poor man. Even as a youth, when he was not yet distinguished by high ecclesiastical or secular office, he alone among all the people of Metz set himself against the pinnacle of imperial majesty for the sake of the liberty of the church. At that time, the kingdom and the church were divided in a most grave schism, which had begun in the days of Emperor Henry III and Pope Gregory VII (earlier called by the name Hildebrand) and which continued through the time of Popes Urban and Paschal, until the time of Pope Calixtus.[2] During this con-

---

1. Alexander III, King of Macedonia and Greece (r. 336–323 BC), is known as "the Great" because of his conquest of Egypt, the Middle East and Persia. Julius Caesar, the Roman dictator murdered in the Senate in 44 BC, was most famous for his conquest of Gaul. Caesar Augustus was the first Roman emperor from 27 BC to AD 14. Charlemagne, the King of the Franks (r. AD 768–814), conquered Saxony and Lombardy and gained the title of emperor in 800. Their heroic deeds were medieval commonplaces.

2. Balderich confuses the origins of the Investiture Controversy, dating it back to the reign of Emperor Henry III (r. 1039–1056), which was well before the pontificate of Gregory VII (r. 1073–1085), who as a

flict, this self-made man undertook to be the defender of Holy Church, a warrior with the wondrous weapons of ingenuity and invention. So that you may understand more completely and clearly why, how, in what way, and to what purpose this man acted in defense of the church against the attacks of the emperor, it seems to me that I must tell why and how this schism occurred.

From the time of Emperor Charlemagne up to the time of Emperor Henry III, kings granted bishoprics through investiture and managed the affairs of churches. This was conceded to them by the Roman pontiffs, both because of the kings' merits, and because the kings both enlarged the churches with gifts and defended them. Henry III, however (whose sins, we hope, have since been veiled over by his many magnificent good works), became extremely infamous for selling bishoprics. For that reason, the aforesaid Pope Gregory VII attempted to take the investiture of bishoprics away from the king.[3] Although he was unable to do so, the pope nevertheless forced the king to firmly promise that he would expel from their sees all those bishops whom he knew to have bought their position for a price, and to grant a bishopric to no person in return for money. When the emperor attempted to carry out this promise, he

---

monk named Hildebrand had served the Roman curia. Henry III had, in fact, enjoyed favorable relations with Rome and helped initiate the reform of the papacy. Passing over Pope Victor III (r. 1086–1087), Balderich lists the reforming popes Urban II (r. 1088–1099), Paschal II (r. 1099–1118) and Calixtus II (r. 1119–1124), who signed the Concordat of Worms with Emperor Henry V in 1122. For more on this dating, see note 4.

3. Gregory VII's conflict was with Henry IV (r. 1056–1106), not with his father Henry III. Gregory threatened to punish Henry IV unless he abstained from contact with those counselors of his who had been excommunicated, stopped interfering in episcopal elections, and obeyed the pope. Instead, Henry called a council of German bishops in January 1076 that declared Gregory deposed. Gregory retaliated by excommunicating and deposing Henry. As a result, many bishops fell away from Henry and made their peace with Rome, while many of the nobility rose up in rebellion. Henry's famous trip to Gregory at Canossa in January 1077 and his absolution and subsequent release from excommunication did not halt the civil war that ensued.

incurred such hatred from almost all the bishops that they allied with Pope Gregory against him, and together with the lord pope they excommunicated him. Many of the cardinals, however, and the Roman clergy as well as the populace, adhered to the king. A great many of their bitter writings against "Pope Hildebrand" still exist.

This Henry was the son of Emperor Conrad.[4] Henry's son, Henry the Elder, inherited his father's conflict with the Roman pontiffs.[5] By imitating his father, he so oppressed these same bishops that through their stratagems and by Roman pontifical authority, he was expelled from his kingdom in the fifty-fourth year of his reign by his son Henry the Younger, and died shortly thereafter in Liège.[6] When Henry the Younger succeeded him to the kingdom, Popes Gregory and Urban had since died, and Pope Paschal, of apostolic memory, reigned. Aflame with godly zeal, Paschal wished to complete what Gregory VII had begun. When Henry the Younger came to Rome for his imperial consecration, the pope refused to anoint him unless Henry gave up his alleged right to episcopal investiture. What result this matter had you can ascertain from a letter

4. This reference to Henry III's father, Emperor Conrad II (r. 1024–1039), confirms Balderich's misunderstanding about the beginnings of the Investiture Controversy. Some of his confusion may derive from the numbering of kings and emperors: in his decrees, Henry III, son of Conrad II, calls himself the third King Henry but, after his imperial coronation, only the second emperor by that name. His son, Henry IV, begins by calling himself the fourth king by the name of Henry, then after his coronation in Rome officially adds "Henry, third august emperor of the Romans." Knowing that the conflict had begun under "Emperor Henry III" Balderich seems to have jumped to the conclusion that this referred to Henry, son of Conrad II, without checking any of the relevant dates.

5. Balderich is referring to Henry IV (r. 1056–1106).

6. It is unclear how Balderich calculated the regnal years, even counting Henry's election as king in 1053, while his father was still alive. Henry V (r. 1106–1125) did depose his father, who died while seeking support for a return to power.

sent throughout the whole kingdom by King Henry as he returned from Rome:[7]

[The Imperial Letter, 1111]

3. "Henry, by the grace of God august emperor of the Romans, to all the faithful of Christ and the church: we wish that it be known to your charity and discernment those things which took place between us and Lord Paschal, how they began, were carried out and accomplished – namely, about the treaty between myself and him, and about the attack of the Romans against me and mine – so that having heard you may understand, having understood you may weigh the evidence, having weighed it you may judge.

"Although at that time I was completely ready to place myself at the service of the church and its wishes, if such were just, the pope began eagerly to promise the enlargement and exaltation of the kingdom beyond that of all my predecessors. Nevertheless, he deviously began to plot how he might tear kingdom and church apart. This was his intention: he wished to take away from our kingdom, without our consent, the investitures of bishops and abbots, a right held since Charlemagne, three hundred and more years, and under sixty-three popes, by their authority and by their confirmation of privileges. And when he was asked by our envoys, what would become of us if all the things upon which our kingdom depends were taken away, since our ancestors had conceded and given almost everything to the churches, he answered: 'Let the brothers of the church be content with their tithes and oblations; let the king, truly, receive and hold for himself and his successors all the treasures and *regalia* which since Charlemagne, Louis, Otto,

---

7. For this famous letter cf. *MGH Constitutiones* 1: nos. 84, 85, 89, 90, 100. The events took place in 1111. See also the translation of Pope Paschal II's letter (below, chapter 6) by E.F. Henderson in Brian Tierney, *The Crisis of Church and State 1050–1300, with Selected Documents* (Englewood Cliffs, NJ, 1964; repr. Toronto, 1988), pp. 89–90.

and Henry have been given to the churches.'[8] To this our envoys responded: 'We do not indeed wish to do violence to the churches lest by taking such a great number of things away from them we incur sacrilege.' And his men affirmed an oath on his behalf that on the Sunday when the 'Esto mihi in Deum'[9] is sung, he would confirm and corroborate all these things, with justice and authority, under penalty of anathema. Likewise we affirmed that if what was promised should be fulfilled – but which the churchmen knew could not possibly be done – I would give up the investitures of the churches, as he sought, just as you can clearly see in the treaty charter.

"As for the attack against us and ours, it transpired this way: we had scarcely entered the gates of the city and were travelling unconcernedly within the walls with our men, when some were wounded, others killed. All the attackers were disarmed and captured. I, however, as though unmoved by so slight a cause, with good and tranquil spirit came up to the doors of Saint Peter with the procession. There, to demonstrate that no offense against God proceeded by our will, I promulgated this decree before the eyes and ears of all present:

[King Henry's Promise to Pope Paschal]

4. " 'I, Henry, by the grace of God august emperor of the Romans, confirm to God and Saint Peter, to all bishops, abbots and all churches, everything which my royal and imperial ancestors conceded or granted to them. And I, a sinner, in fear of terrible judgment, refuse to take back in any way those things which they offered to God in hope of eternal re-

---

8. The term *regalia* includes both parcels of land as well as political, legal, and judicial authority over those who live there. See Chapters 5 and 6 for sample lists of such rights. The German kings delegated these royal possessions and prerogatives to the prince-bishops, thereby giving them substantial political authority.

9. *Esto mihi in Deum* is the introit sung on the seventh Sunday before Easter, which in 1111 fell on 12 February.

ward.' This being decreed and signed by me, I petitioned the pope that he fulfill for me exactly what was written in the treaty charter. This was his treaty charter to me:

[The Papal Promise to King Henry]

5. " 'The lord pope shall order all those bishops present on the day of the king's coronation to return to the king the *regalia*, and to the kingdom those things that have pertained to the kingdom from the time of Charlemagne, Louis, Otto and Henry and all his other predecessors. And he will confirm this in writing under penalty of anathema, lest anyone present or absent or their successors should assume or usurp the same *regalia*, i.e. cities, duchies, marches, counties, mints, tolls, markets, advocacies, all rights of hundred courts, i.e. of bailiffs, manors and villages which belonged to the realm, along with all their appurtenances, armies and castles. Neither shall the lord pope trouble the king or the kingdom further about these matters, and he will confirm them by a privilege under penalty of anathema so that his successors may not attempt further trouble. He will receive the king favorably and honorably; and with no usage of his catholic predecessors knowingly omitted, he shall crown the king; and with the aid of his office he will help the king to hold to all these things. If the lord pope fails to fulfill these promises for the king, I, Peter Leonis, swear that with my total power I will side with the lord king.[10] The hostages, however (unless they have fled), we will return on the day after the king's coronation. Likewise we will return them, if, through any fault of the pope, he is not crowned. On the Sunday when the king arrives in procession, I will give as hostages my son Gratian, and my grandson Wizo or the son of my sister, if I am able to have him. These are the oaths: 'I, Peter Leonis, swear to you that next Sunday the lord pope will fulfill to the king what is

10. Peter Leonis or Pierleone (d. 1116) was the prefect or chief lay administrator of Rome.

written in the treaty charter.' These are the oaths on our part: 'I, Count Herman,' 'I, Count Godfrey,' 'I, Count Frederick,' 'I, Folmar,' 'I, Chancellor Adalbert, swear to you that on the next Wednesday or Thursday the lord king shall make the princes swear thus and shall render hostages, just as is written in the treaty charter.'

"When, therefore, I insisted upon the above-mentioned request, namely that the lord pope confirm with justice and authority the treaty promised to me, even while everyone (namely the bishops and abbots, both his and ours, and all sons of the church) was protesting to his face and claiming his decree amounted to open heresy, he was willing to offer the following privilege – if without violating the peace of the church one can call it such:

[Pope Paschal's Privilege for King Henry]
6. " 'Bishop Paschal, servant of the servants of God, to his beloved son King Henry and his successors: It is forbidden by the institution of divine law and interdicted by the sacred canons that priests should occupy themselves with secular business, or go to the public court except to rescue the condemned or to aid those who suffer injury. Whence also the Apostle Paul says: "If then you have judgments of secular cases, set them to judge who are least esteemed in the church."[11] In parts of your kingdom, however, bishops and abbots are so occupied with secular concerns that they are compelled to frequent the public court and perform military service assiduously, which things rarely, if ever, are done without pillage, sacrilege, arson or murder. The ministers of the altar are thereby made into ministers of the court, since they accept from kings, cities, duchies, marches, mints, tolls, manors and other things pertaining to the service of the kingdom.

" 'Whence the custom has grown intolerable for the church that elected bishops cannot accept consecration, unless they are first invested by the royal hand. For this

11. 1 Cor 6:4.

reason both ambition and the depravity of simoniac heresy have sometimes prevailed to such an extent that episcopal sees were usurped without any election. Indeed, sometimes they have been invested while the previous bishops still lived. Provoked by these and many other evils which pertained mostly to investiture, our predecessors Gregory VII and Urban II, pontiffs of blessed memory, condemned these investitures by the lay hand at frequently convened episcopal councils. And they determined that if any clerics had obtained churches in that fashion, they should be deposed and the givers of the churches should also be deprived of communion, according to that chapter of the apostolic canons which runs: 'If any bishop should obtain a church by the powers of secular usage, he shall be deposed and cast out together with all those who associate with him.'[12] Following their lead, we have confirmed their sentence in an episcopal council.

" 'To you, therefore, dearest son, Henry, King, and now through our office by the grace of God Emperor of the Romans, and also to your kingdom we decree the return of those *regalia* which manifestly pertained to the kingdom in the time of Charlemagne, Louis, and your other predecessors. Indeed, we forbid and prohibit, under pain of anathema, that any bishop or abbot, present or future, usurp these *regalia*, i.e. cities, duchies, marches, counties, mints, tolls, markets, advocacies, rights of hundred courts, manors which belonged to the kingdom, along with their appurtenances, armies and castles. Nor shall they hereafter be admitted to these *regalia* except through permission of the king. Neither shall it be permitted that those who succeed us in the apostolic see trouble either you or your kingdom concerning this matter.

" 'Further we decree that the churches, with their offerings to God and hereditary possessions that clearly did not

12. This canon was codified in Gratian's *Decretum*, pars prima, distinctio 63, causa 7.

belong to the kingdom, remain free, just as you promised on the day of your coronation to the Almighty Lord in the sight of the whole church. It is fitting that the bishops, freed from secular concerns, should take care of their people, and no longer be absent from their churches. For according to the Apostle Paul, "Let them be vigilant, for they shall render account for the souls of their people."[13]

[More on the Investiture Controversy]

7. As you may deduce from the tenor of the letter, dear reader, this was not the end of the matter. But so great a discord over it divided those who were there with the king that a bitter battle broke out on the steps of Saint Peter between the king's army and the Roman populace. Then the king captured the pope, taking him and certain cardinals away to Viterbo. There the king, so it is said, while he was looking at paintings in the church, saw one depicting Jacob wrestling with the angel. He pointed this painting out to the lord pope, saying as did Jacob: "I will not let you go, unless you bless me."[14] And so he extorted by force from the lord pope not only the imperial unction, but also oaths that the pope would never pronounce a sentence of excommunication against him. Since the lord pope as a God-fearing man firmly kept these promises, the prelates of the church, mourning their pious father's misfortune, avoided the company of the emperor. Thus we had the emperor versus the churches, the churches versus the emperor.

But perhaps, dear reader, you will mock me with the words of Horace: "He started to make an amphora; the wheel is now turning, why is a pitcher coming out?"[15] By this I mean that, although I promised to relate the deeds of

13. Cf. Hebr 13:17: "Obey your leaders and submit to them: for they are keeping watch over your souls, as men who will have to give account. Let them do this joyfully, and not sadly: for that would be of no advantage to you."

14. Gen 32: 26.

15. Horace, *Ars poetica* 21.

Albero, I turned my attention to the actions of Roman pontiffs and of kings. But I simply reply to you using words of the same Horace: "The beginning is not inconsistent with the middle, nor the middle with the end."[16]

[Albero's Struggle for the Liberty of the Church]
8. For at that time lord Albero, cleric of Metz, alone amongst all, or rather in opposition to all in Metz, stood by the lord pope; and undaunted, he accomplished many things through his quick wit and resolution for the honor and service of the lord pope and for the liberty of the universal church. Accordingly, he also aroused against himself the most severe outbursts of royal displeasure, which he nonetheless most frequently evaded by virtue of his wonderful ingenuity.

[The Interdict on Metz, 1116/7]
9. Since the king allowed the churches no freedom to elect bishops, likewise on his own authority he set up as bishop in the city of Metz a certain nobleman by the name of Adalberon, after that venerable man, Bishop Poppo, had been expelled from his see.[17] The aforesaid lord Albero, by often travelling to Rome, caused Adalberon to be deposed and finally excommunicated, so that Adalberon died excommunicate and was buried outside the church.[18]

And through an apostolic rescript, Albero gained an interdict against divine offices in the city, which prohibited even burial for the dead.[19] Fearing a most cruel death, no

16. Ibid., 152.
17. Poppo's election in 1090 was disputed by Henry IV, who set up his own candidate, Adalberon IV (r. 1090–1121). With the support of the majority of the citizens of Metz, Adalberon drove Poppo out of the city in about 1097. Poppo died in exile ca. 1103.
18. Albero succeeded in having Adalberon deposed in late 1116 or early 1117. Nonetheless, Adalberon managed to defy his enemies until his death, probably sometime in 1121.
19. Interdicts prohibited all religious services throughout a territory. Without access to the sacraments, people feared for their souls and were supposed to press rulers to obtain forgiveness from ecclesiastical authorities.

one dared to bring back to Metz the letters of the lord pope containing the sentence of interdict. Therefore, Albero donned a cleric's linen robe, covered his head and face with a woman's veil, put on a cloak of unbleached cloth, and in the guise of a female pilgrim bearing frankincense to the altar, he placed the papal letters upon it. And then turning around, he summoned the canons, whom he saw in that church of Saint Stephan, and ordered them to take the papal letters from the altar and reverently read them. As soon as they recognized Albero, however, they raged and shouted and hurried to arouse the people of the city against him by ringing the church bells. But before they were able to seize him, he quickly jumped onto a horse, which he had ready in front of the church doors, and fled at full speed. Although the citizens of Metz, both on foot and on horseback, pursued him all the way to the village of Argancy, Albero crossed the Mosel river on the brave horse which he was riding and came to his lord at castle Rozei, located in the patrimonial estate of his bishop, Poppo.[20] By similar means he many times escaped the king's snares.

[Albero's Escape to Rome]
10. The king, meanwhile, had blocked all the roads and instructed all his vassals to kill Albero as he journeyed to Rome. For the king had publicly pronounced Albero an adversary and enemy of the kingdom. Albero, however, passed unrecognized through the midst of his enemies, by transforming himself into many guises. Once he dressed his servants in his own clothing and ministered to them in servant's garb: he attended to the horses, prepared the meals, took their boots off, and ate the servants' scraps. One time he went among beggars as a beggar, another time among merchants as if bearing merchandise; and in countless other ways he would disguise himself, not just by

---

20. Argancy is just north of Metz; castle Rozei is unknown.

changing clothing, but also by coloring his face, hair and beard with dye.

It is also said, although I do not know for sure, that once while disguised as a cripple seated upon an ass, he came upon the king and his army and accepted five shillings in alms from the queen.[21] It is also added, but I do not know first hand, that on this same journey Albero accompanied the king's procession for a while, and, in the guise of a beggar at the foot of the royal table, heard the king freely discussing many details with the queen and his other vassals about the things he was planning against the pope. And among other things, the king listed the traps laid against lord Albero himself, both how many and which roads were closed against him on his way to Rome. Thus forewarned, Albero evaded all the king's snares, and arriving at Rome, he sent to the queen many and great thanks for the gift he had received from her; he confided that he was the one seated on an ass to whom she had given five shillings.

And when the king discovered that Albero had arrived in Rome, he prepared traps for him not only by land, but also by sea, so that Albero would in no way be able to escape him on his way back. But none of this was hidden from lord Albero. And so while he was returning from Rome, he came to Pisa. Knowing that the king had ordered the Pisans to kill him, he did not dare to enter the seaport as himself. Just in case the king's men were already lying in wait for him there, his servant engaged a ship for himself and for a companion whom the servant pretended would presently be coming. But on the day when the ship that had been hired was supposed to set sail, his servant boarded the ship with the baggage. Albero himself, however, did not dare board the ship, since there was a great crowd of people in the port to see the sights, and he feared that those lying in wait for him might be among them. So he set

21. A reference to Empress Mathilda or Maud, wife of Henry V, the daughter of King Henry I of England (r. 1100–1135).

out to sea from another place aboard a small fishing boat that had been acquired earlier and pursued the ship, just catching up to it on the same day. Yet when he attempted to board the ship, he fell into the sea and floundered in the water for a while until finally he was with difficulty hauled aboard with a rope thrown from the poop deck.

In the evening, when his clothing had dried and he was eating with the sailors, they began to notice his very delicate hands and realized from this that he was not a commoner. The sailors had been forced by the Pisans to swear that they would take no one on board their ship carrying apostolic letters. Accordingly, they told Albero they wished to inspect his bags, in case he might be carrying letters against the lord emperor. And they told him how they had received this order from the Pisans and had given their word. But lord Albero had hidden the letters in a carved ivory box, which he had wrapped appropriately in a purple cloth, just like a sacred object. He told the sailors that the box contained the relics of saints, which he was bringing from lands across the sea. He also added that when he was floundering in the sea, it was their support that had saved him from the danger of drowning. Whereupon the sailors were overawed, and showing reverence to the sacred object, they did not dare open it. Thus did Albero escape these and many other perils.

[Disguised in Strasbourg]
11. Another time in the bishopric of Strasbourg, he knew that royal agents had laid snares for him along the road he was to travel and that he could not avoid them. And so dressing himself in military attire complete with shield and lance and riding on a powerful horse, he quickly rode up into their midst and abruptly asked them if they had seen Albero, "the Devil of Metz," passing by there, for the king had sent him to capture Albero at once. And he cursed Albero, saying: "May God grant him as many evil hours as I

have spent all night following him." Thus by a thousand stratagems he often eluded the snares of the king.

[Albero and Metz]

12. During the time of this discord the citizens of Metz twice destroyed the house which he had in their city, and scattered his goods. But he himself also forced them twice to rebuild the house and restore his stolen goods.

[Albero and Count Rainald, 1118–1120]

13. When the aforesaid Bishop Poppo finally died, Albero without royal permission arranged for Metz to have as bishop a certain man of extraordinary sanctity. But although this bishop had been consecrated, the city would not let him enter, and within a few days he was translated to his residence in the Eternal City.[22]

After this man, Albero made the people of Metz accept a bishop by the name of Stephan, brother of Count Rainald of Mousson.[23] It was believed that Albero did this out of love for Count Rainald, because the two seemed to be as one, equal through their friendship. During the time of the aforesaid discord, the count had made his castle at Mousson available to Albero so that Albero could make war against Metz from there. From that castle, at one time Albero secretly entered the city and hid in the home of a certain widow. In the morning, he suddenly mounted his horse and showed himself in the streets. When he was recognized, a great clamor arose throughout the entire city,

22. 'Translation' is the technical term for a change of bishopric. The Eternal City refers to heaven. It was, in fact, long after Poppo's death in 1103 that Theotger or Dietger (r. 1118–1120), who had been Abbot of St. Georgen in the Black Forest, was elected bishop. Theotger never gained any real support and never entered Metz.

23. Stephan von Bar was Bishop of Metz from 1120 to 1163. The Counts of Mousson, who later called themselves the Counts of Bar, were powerful in Toul and even managed to expand their power into Verdun. Their support, therefore, was essential in establishing Stephan in Metz. Stephan's connection to his uncle, Pope Calixtus II, also may have helped.

and whoever had a horse pursued him for a great distance outside the city. Count Rainald, however, had his knights ready in ambush, just as he and lord Albero had arranged, and attacking the Metz citizens, he captured many of them.

Later, however, it transpired that Count Rainald allied himself with the citizens of Metz, after accepting gifts which would have dazzled the hearts of wise men; and he broke off his friendship with lord Albero. Albero was outraged at this betrayal and harshly threatened the count to his face, openly predicting that great dishonor would come to him because of this act. Then, right in front of the count, Albero ordered his horse to be saddled and hastened to King Henry, into whose full grace he had recently returned. Through much persuasion Albero brought it about that the king himself came to Mousson, and when the king had besieged it, the count fled by night and escaped to Bar-le-Duc.[24] The king, however, left Mousson and encircled Bar with a great army. Then he compelled the count to surrender and took him captive. But afterwards, swayed by many pleadings, lord Albero restored to the count his freedom and gained his acquittal. Finally, their friendship, which for a time had been shattered, became so constant and firm that no cause, not even death, could break it.

[Albero's Church Offices]

14. Already in those days lord Albero had accumulated many offices and incomes, for he had been made *primicerius* of the church of Metz, and archdeacon and provost of Saint Arnual.[25] He had also obtained an archdeaconate

24. Count Rainald (r. 1105–1149) was besieged and then briefly imprisoned by the king in 1113 as the result of a territorial dispute between the count and the Bishop of Verdun. Balderich's placement of Albero at the center of events is improbable, in view of Albero's continuing poor relations with the king until the Concordat of Worms in 1122.

25. *Primicerius* is a rare title, probably equivalent to a chancellor for bishop and chapter. The village of St. Arnual is now incorporated into the city of Saarbrücken.

in the church of Verdun, and in the church of Toul, where
he had been born, he was archdeacon and provost of Saint
Gengoult. As I just said, he was born in the bishopric of
Toul to noble parents.[26] And in that bishopric, before he
was elected by the citizens of Trier, he built an abbey on his
paternal estate which was called Montreuil. There he
brought together men of great religion and sanctity as regu-
lar canons. The abbey is called Belchamp.[27] In our times,
indeed, no one strove with greater purpose to attract religious and literate men around him and to esteem them and
honor them abundantly with gifts. Moreover, Albero was
always hospitable, above and beyond his financial resources, and he also was wont to treat strangers pleasantly
and humanely.

[Elections in Magdeburg, Halberstadt and Trier, 1126–1131]
15. While these things were happening, he was elected to the
archbishopric of Magdeburg in the time of King and Emperor
Lothar III.[28] But he refused the office in every way and ingeniously brought it about that Lord Norbert, a man of renowned piety, assumed the leadership of that church.

Also during the same emperor's reign, Albero came to
Halberstadt just when that city's clergy had convened to elect
a bishop to the vacant see.[29] And since opinions were divided, they could not decide upon any one person. When they

26. His parents were Lord Gérard and Adelaide of Montreuil-
Thicourt. His brother, Peter, shared in the foundation of Belchamp.
27. Belchamp was built in the neighborhood of Bayon, Lunéville.
Little remains of the abbey today.
28. Duke Lothar von Supplinburg of Saxony was king from 1125 to
1137, adding the imperial title in 1133. Although Lothar numbered himself "*tercius*" or "the third" as both king and emperor, the manuscript
mistakenly calls him "*secundum*" or "the second." Saint Norbert of
Xanten founded the Premonstratentian Order in the 1120s; he was Archbishop of Magdeburg from 1126 to 1134. Balderich exaggerates Magdeburg's attempt to elect Albero and Albero's role in Norbert's election.
29. These events took place in 1129, when Bishop Otto (r. 1123–
1135) had been briefly removed from power by reform-minded clergy in
his diocese.

heard that such a great and worthy man had arrived, they all unanimously agreed upon Albero. But when Albero learned this, he abandoned his mid-day meal, which had just been prepared for him in the house of a certain venerable person (Chamberlain Conrad, whom King Henry had had blinded during the time of the aforesaid schism).[30] And just as his servants had begun to wash their hands and were about to go in for their meal, he unexpectedly mounted a horse and ordered them to follow him immediately; and so he fled.

Finally, during the reigns of lord Pope Innocent and King Lothar, the clergy of Trier, against the wishes of all laymen, elected Albero archbishop.[31] In what manner the election was accomplished, however, you may deduce from the tenor of the letter below, which the clergy sent to lord Pope Innocent. Here is the letter:

"To the most blessed pontiff of the Catholic Church, the people of the Church of Trier render devoted servitude of obedience and service. It has not escaped your notice, reverend father, how for these past two years the Church of Trier has been deprived of a pastor of its own. And you know also that we have not been able to secure lord Bruno, whom we elected unanimously.[32] But passing over the hardships and travails which we have endured in the meantime, we make known to you new dire straits and perils, an end to which we desire to obtain as soon as possible through your paternal aid.

"An assembly was indeed held to elect a pastor when the king was in our city, and with him lord Albano, also the bishops of Metz and Toul, and the barons of our province.

30. Nothing else is known of this cathedral chamberlain of Halberstadt.
31. These events took place in 1130–1131. Innocent II's pontificate lasted from 1130 to 1143.
32. Bruno von Berg, with papal permission, refused the archbishopric of Trier in December 1130, apparently because he expected to be elected Archbishop of Cologne, which was across the Rhine from Altenberg, the castle of the Counts von Berg. As Balderich explains in Chapter 16, Bruno was elected Archbishop of Cologne and reigned there from 1131 to 1137.

We nominated five candidates, so that one of them might more easily be chosen by common consent.[33] After these five were nominated, the barons and all the laymen (after first withdrawing from us to take counsel and then returning to us) requested none of the five named, but rather they all, with one voice, requested one Gebhard of Würzburg.[34] Although we demonstrated just cause for his rejection, nevertheless by shouting and making a disturbance, they persevered in their request to such an extent that many of our brothers began to agree with them. So the meeting dissolved for that day, its business unfinished.

"But afterwards, a few of us, not sufficiently confident in our powers against such a great number, sought counsel from the bishops, namely of Albano and Metz. And finally we placed ourselves and our cause in their hands and counsel [agreeing] that we would elect whatever person they resolved upon, provided that he would be acceptable to you, father, and that the lord king would be willing to invest him. What happened? Albano and Metz spoke to the king. Then, returning to us, they advised us to elect lord Albero, *primicerius* of Metz. And they said Albero was pleasing to the lord king and that the king's favor would be with us in this matter. Moved, therefore, by this assurance, we then convened to hold the election. When the Palatine Count (who is the advocate of our church) and the other nobles and the people became aware of our intention, they made such a disturbance and tumult that they threw us into complete disorder. And then all of them demanded the appointment of lord Godfrey, provost of our church, who had

33. King Lothar was in Trier at Easter 1131 with Cardinal Matthew of Albano (r. 1127–1135) and Bishop Henry of Toul (r. 1126–1165), as well as local nobility like the Count Palatine William (d. 1140), Count Conrad of Luxemburg and Otto von Rheineck.

34. Gebhard von Henneburg (d. 1159) was first named Bishop of Würzburg in 1121, but in 1126, during a conflict over the diocese, the pope excommunicated and deposed him. He regained the see in 1150.

been the first among the original five nominations. But since we had been pledged to Albero, as was said above, we refused to grant their request and deferred the election until after the departure of the king and barons. For in their presence, we did not dare to elect the *primicerius*. Then, while he was leaving, the king designated a day for us at Mainz, affirming that he wished to deal with our business there by a decision of the bishops.[35]

"Meanwhile, we few (namely the provost of the cathedral, the dean, two archdeacons, the provost of Saint Paulin, the school master, the sexton and four other cathedral canons) convened in our choir and elected lord Albero, with the hope that he would be pleasing to you, lord father, and that the lord king, as is his given right, would be willing to invest him, just as the bishops of Albano and Metz had promised us. In fact, we knew, and we know better even now, that by no means, through no cleverness, could the anger and rage of the laymen be assuaged, except by royal power and grace. The reason we did not call more brothers to the election, moreover, was out of fear: we feared our fellow citizens, who might have rushed in to murder us, if by chance they found out about our actions; and we had little hope of the assent of some of our brothers, since we had earlier seen that, frightened by the fear of death (so we believe), they supported the laymen. And yet, at the time many of our brothers accepted our report of the election with friendly mind and words.

"But afterwards, when we arrived in Mainz on the appointed day and presented the results of the election to the lord king, he was swayed by partiality for the laymen, and neither heard us with the hoped-for good-will, nor took up our cause. And when the king was at last reminded by the lord of Albano of the aforesaid promise, he declared before all the bishops and princes who were present that he had never promised Albano or Metz that

35. The meeting in Mainz took place in late June or July 1131.

he favored the election of any person, unless the choice could be made with the agreement and assent of all the people, both laymen and clerics.

"Thus we departed from the king both confused and frustrated. And now that we have returned home, we find that almost all the clerics, except for those of us who made the election, are at odds with us. And whenever we speak with them and try to vindicate ourselves, they allege as their excuse their fear for the destruction of cloisters, the seizure of their prebends, and the peril of their lives. And they complain that they can find no remedy for all their misfortunes.

"Therefore, throwing ourselves at the feet of Your Majesty, through the love of Jesus Christ we implore that you quickly gain the king's approval, which the lords of Albano and Metz promised to us. Otherwise, all that remains is either that you restore to us our first bishop-elect, namely lord Bruno, or else, without violating your paternal grace, we will unavoidably have to elect another person, upon whom the wishes of clergy and people may agree. We are not, to be sure, motivated merely by the evils which we endure and expect to have to endure, but also by the constant wails of our brothers, clerics, monks, nuns, orphans and widows, and their complaints that it is our fault that they are wretchedly exposed to all dangers."

[Opposition to Albero's Election]
16. As you can see from the tenor of this letter, laymen (both freemen and ministerials) opposed the election of Albero. Among them, Ludwig, a certain burgrave, the prefect of the city, a man from the household of the church, broke into the homes of all those clerics who did not oppose Albero's election and seized all their possessions.[36]

36. Ludwig de Ponte was a ministerial, one of the legally unfree laymen who served the archbishops as administrators and warriors. As pre-

And furthermore, what is even more cruel, by the bridge at Konz they laid in wait for all the most excellent clerics of the church and those honored with higher offices who were hastening to Metz to demand the [consecration of the] bishop-elect.[37] These laymen stripped the clerics of their vestments and horses; and, horrible to say, they even frightened and disturbed these noble persons with fearful blows and beatings.

We ought to commemorate the names of those who endeavored to defend the liberty of the church. These, then, were the active and energetic men, tested in tribulation and constant in faith: the Cathedral Provost Godfrey, Dean Folmar, Archdeacon Arnulf, Archdeacons Theodore and Bolso, also lord Hillin (still at that time subdeacon, who was the immediate successor to the aforesaid lord Albero in the archiepiscopal see), and lord Bruno.[38]

Bruno, the brother of Count Adolf von Berg, was then provost of Coblenz and afterwards became Archbishop of Cologne. At the time of this tribulation, all of Trier had unanimously elected Bruno archbishop, before they nominated lord Albero. But Bruno, through much labor, obtained his release from lord Pope Innocent by presenting certain secret grounds. Moreover, it was said that he was not willing to accept the honor offered him out of a desire for a richer bishopric (albeit one of lesser dignity). And indeed he subsequently proved this to be the case. For a short time later, when Bruno was studying in France, the clergy and people of Cologne by universal consent elected a certain Godfrey, Provost of Xanten. Upon learning this news, Bruno immediately returned; and after he had caused Godfrey's election to be annulled, he accepted that same bishopric.

---

fect or burgrave (the military commander for the city) Ludwig had attained a great deal of power in Trier.

37. The bridge crossed the Saar river, south of Trier.

38. Hillin von Falmagne (r. 1152–1169) succeeded Albero as Archbishop of Trier.

[Albero Becomes Archbishop and Enters Trier, 1131–1132]
17. While all this was happening, it transpired that a council presided over by Pope Innocent was convened at the city of Rheims.[39] At that council, the lord Albero and the clerics of Trier came together with opposing intentions: the latter were striving to overcome the reluctance of their elected candidate through the pope's coercion; the former was struggling to be released from this burden and recover the offices and ecclesiastical benefices which he had lost because of his disobedience. (When Albero still persisted in declining this burden having been repeatedly ordered by the pope to accept it, Pope Innocent had suspended Albero from every one of his ecclesiastical offices and benefices.) And so, at this council, the lord pope ordered Albero to be raised on high and, attired with a cope, to be placed among the archbishops. And then leading him to Vienne, even though he still petitioned for his release, the pope consecrated him archbishop there.[40]

When news of this reached Trier, Ludwig, the aforesaid burgrave, instigated a conspiracy, vowing that if ever lord Albero should enter the city of Trier, the conspirators would kill him. And Ludwig added this oath: that he himself would be the first to attack Albero. The reason Ludwig opposed lord Albero to such a degree was this: by his cunning Ludwig had Archbishop Godfrey so much under his control that Ludwig claimed that he himself held in benefice the palace and all its episcopal revenues, that it was his duty to provide for the bishop and his chaplains, and that he held in benefice all the other things pertaining to the bishopric. Ludwig said, further, that the celebrating of masses, clerical ordinations, and church consecrations pertained to the bishop; indeed, he declared it was within his right to rule the land, to dispose all matters in the

39. The council took place at the end of October and early November 1131.
40. His consecration took place in early March 1132.

bishopric, and to keep an army. Accordingly, every day he served one pint of wine and two pints of beer for the bishop's meal, while he daily feasted splendidly with a multitude of men at his own table, like a great prince. And he went everywhere surrounded by a troop of soldiers and in all ways lorded it over the whole land.

Consequently, Bishop Godfrey was greatly hated by all the clerics, because, spurning the counsel and friendship of the whole clergy, he devoted himself wholly to laymen. The clerics, therefore, began to work to depose him. Oppressed by poverty, Godfrey succumbed to his adversaries.[41] The aforesaid Ludwig had deprived Godfrey not just of wealth, but also of his wisdom and reason. For Godfrey was wanting in both, as often happens when a person who ought to be intent on the public welfare instead transfers all his cares and anxieties to someone else, lazily wishing to remain idle in indolent slothfulness and not willing to be bothered either with respect to himself or anyone else. As it says in the proverb:[42] "Your rucksack you may give to your servant, but keep the prudence of your counsel deep within yourself." (King Childerich of the Franks was deposed from his kingdom for a similar reason, and the kingdom was given, with the approval of Pope Hadrian, to the man to whom Childerich had entrusted its governance, namely Pippin, the mayor of the palace.)[43] And because Ludwig knew Albero was a man of sharp wit and prepared for anything and would not be subservient to him, and because he had learned that Albero would not tolerate being lorded

41. The weak Archbishop Godfrey von Falmagne of Trier (r. 1124–1127) was eventually deposed because of simony.

42. The source of the proverb is unknown.

43. In 751 Pippin became the first Carolingian king when he deposed Childerich III, the last of the Merovingians. As mayors of the palace the Carolingians had been running the Frankish kingdom in all but name for several generations. The pope who supported the transfer was Zacharius (r. 741–752) and not Hadrian (r. 772–795).

over but would himself be lord, for these reasons Ludwig opposed him.

Do you want to hear the end of this matter? Listen: "Neither does the ox love his yoke; nonetheless what he hates, he has."⁴⁴ When this sworn conspiracy was made known to him, at first Archbishop Albero stayed away from the city entrusted to him, as if avoiding the burden of archiepiscopal office. Then, not unlike a river which, blocked by an obstacle, at first flows silently and calmly in its course, then, as if no longer able to endure the obstacle's resistance, with a tumultuous roar and crashing waves wears down its banks and bursts its confines, so too this invincible and fearless man collected a great army, and approached Trier. Trier's clerics in solemn procession met him at the Porta Alba and showing great friendliness received him with hymns and praises.⁴⁵ Ludwig and his fellow conspirators likewise met him there, but when they saw him surrounded by such a large troop of soldiers, astounded and confused in mind, they immediately feigned peaceful intentions. And Ludwig hastened to be the first among them to pay respects to his lord in a fawning and humble voice and approached him for the kiss of peace.

[Investiture by King Lothar]
18. It should not be omitted that when Archbishop Albero had come to the imperial court in Aachen, King Lothar was not willing to invest him with the *regalia*, since Albero had received the episcopal consecration before he had requested his investiture.⁴⁶ And so it was believed that the king himself would have utterly opposed Albero, except that he knew that Albero was a great man, who could easily

44. Ovid, *Amores* 3.11.36.
45. The Porta Alba was a gate in the old Roman wall on the south side of the city, by the church of St. Alba.
46. The court was held during Easter in April 1132. Episcopal conescration prior to investiture with the *regalia* was, of course, in explicit violation of the Concordat of Worms.

have aroused the whole territory of his empire against him. Therefore, the king accepted a facile explanation from Albero: by common counsel of the princes Albero swore an oath to the king: that he had not accepted consecration intending any diminution of royal honor, but rather because he was compelled by the lord pope to do so. The lord king accepted his oath, and with the royal scepter granted to him the *regalia*. Also during the same court, Albero excommunicated Duke Simon of Lotharingia, the king's brother; and on Easter Sunday, while the gospel was being read, Albero forced the duke to leave the church.[47]

[Albero vs. Ludwig de Ponte]
19. Neither should it be passed over in silence that after having accepted the *regalia*, Albero was about to enter Trier, but not so much could be found from among all the episcopal incomes from which provisions for the first day could be prepared for him. In fact, everything pertaining to the episcopate was either pawned or the aforesaid Ludwig and his fellow conspirators claimed that they held it in benefice. For this reason, Albero had made preparations against poverty beforehand: the lord archbishop had procured permission from Pope Innocent that, for the space of three years after his consecration, he be allowed to hold the ecclesiastical incomes which he had held before his episcopacy. And since, according to previous practice, Albero's wine, grain and everything else pertaining to his provisions was brought to the palace, Ludwig had it all locked up, every day allotting to Albero no more than was pleasing to him, just as he had done with Albero's predecessors. The rest Ludwig consumed with his own men.

Although the lord archbishop tolerated this for a while, Ludwig exhausted his patience too far: one afternoon when

47. This took place on 10 April 1132. Duke Simon I (r. 1115–1139), a stepbrother of the king, had encroached on the prerogatives of a church in Toul. He later repented, and Albero then lifted the excommunication.

certain foreigners had come to the archiepiscopal court, as was customary, Albero commanded his guests to be feted. Yet when his servants went to the palace for the wine, Ludwig's steward responded that he could give nothing to them unless lord Ludwig had ordered him. Since Albero had often suffered this and similar things, this evil finally seemed to him intolerable.

Consequently, at great expense he rebuilt Pfalzel, Julius Caesar's castle located near the city, which was at that time dilapidated and uninhabitable,[48] and he ordered provisions to be brought there. And then he offered this taunt: "Let Ludwig have his palace now!" In residence there for the next three years, Albero directed his whole attention to freeing the episcopal revenues. He redeemed for 300 marks the manor at Humbach, which his predecessor lord Meginher had mortgaged.[49] And lord Albero redeemed almost all the other holdings pertaining to the episcopate which had either been mortgaged or given in benefice by Archbishop Godfrey. Maintaining the empty palace at his own expense, Ludwig finally reached such a state of humiliation that, in bare feet and sackcloth, he threw himself at the feet of the archbishop at Pfalzel, pleading for mercy and giving the palace back to Albero.

[King Lothar, Castle Arras and King Conrad, 1136–1139]
20. In those days the lord archbishop had become exceedingly rich in material goods by accumulating many things, and with these increasing everyday, he was making preparations for certain great plans which he had in mind. Knowing that, in conformity with the venerable privileges of his church, the Abbey of Saint Maximin was located on

48. Pfalzel lay just across the Mosel from Trier. It was built not by Julius Caesar but during the fourth century as part of an imperial palace and fortification complex.

49. Meginher was archbishop from 1127 to 1130. Humbach later became the important center of Montabaur, which a mainstay of the archiepiscopal territory on the right bank of the Rhine.

land belonging to St. Peter's Cathedral in Trier and therefore pertained to his disposition by ancient right, Albero directed his full attention as to how he might remove the abbey from the power of the king and restore it to his church. Toward that end, he set out on the expedition to Italy with King Lothar, officially with 100 knights according to his assessment, but in reality with only 67.[50] And after King Roger of Sicily had been expelled from the borders of Apulia, which he had occupied, Apulia had been given to Duke Rainald, and the *regalia* of blessed Peter had been recovered, the emperor was returning home when he succumbed to the common fate of mortals in the valley of Trent.

The lord archbishop, however, after being decorated by lord Pope Innocent with the office of papal legate, was on his way home when, coming to Remiremont, he heard news that Count Otto von Rheineck, a member of the royal army in Italy, had commanded two brothers, Werner and John von Nantersburg, to capture Albero's castle of Arras through treachery.[51] And when this was accomplished, the castle was to be removed [from the archbishop's authority]. Although Albero desired rest after his many labors, he now saw that many great troubles were threatening him again.

50. Lothar entered Italy in 1136 to assert his imperial prerogatives and support Pope Innocent II against the incursions of the Norman King Roger II (r. 1105–1154) of Sicily, who was himself supported by the antipope Anacletus II (r. 1130–1138). Though the campaign was successful, the pope and emperor quarreled over who should control the spoils, which led to their joint investiture of Count Rainald or Rainulf of Alife (d. 1139) with Apulia. Tired of the fighting, Lothar broke off the campaign and was on his way back to Germany when he suddenly died on 4 December 1137.

51. Otto von Rheineck (d. 1150) had been trying since 1136 to expand his power by claiming the title of Count Palatine by the Rhine. For more on that struggle, see Chapter 30. Here Otto is defying his feudal lord for this castle, namely Albero, and trying to become sole feudal lord himself, with the right to enfeoff his own vassals. Compare this incident to Chapter 26, for Albero's ongoing difficulty in maintaining his suzerainty over Arras. The castle Nantersburg (now called Entersburg) and castle Arras both lay east of Wittlich.

Manfully making his spirit firm against adversity, he swore by his tonsure that he would not shave his beard until he had recovered his castle Arras and had destroyed Nantersburg, the castle of those brothers Werner and John. Assembling all princes of the land of Toul and Metz, he came to Trier with a great army and simultaneously besieged both castles, namely Arras and Nantersburg. And having destroyed Nantersburg and regained Arras, he returned to Trier in great triumph.

It should also not go unnoticed that while returning from the Italian expedition, the aforesaid lord Albero forcibly carried off from Parma the relics of his predecessor, Archbishop Meginher, and brought them with him to Trier. The aforesaid Meginher, great-souled man that he was, excommunicated Conrad (later king) when he had been elevated over Lothar.[52] And so the same lord Conrad (afterwards king) captured Meginher as he was hastening to Rome on church business and held him for ransom in Parma for a great sum of money. Meginher died there in prison.

But the same Conrad, having at that time been elevated to king, reconciled with King Lothar on that expedition. He also befriended and aided Archbishop Albero, because he saw the strength and spirit of the kingdom manifested in him. And they were united in such friendship that after the death of emperor Lothar, Albero worked with all his energy and against almost all the princes of the kingdom had

52. Archbishop Meginher showed his loyalty to King Lothar by excommunicating Conrad von Staufen, who had claimed the kingship from 1127 to 1135. Lothar had been elected king, although the Staufen were the legal heirs of the Salian, the last royal dynasty. Disputes between the Staufen and King Lothar over rights to the crown possessions led to war and to Conrad's rival kingship. This was the origin of the long-lasting conflict between the Staufen/Waiblingen and the Welf/Guelph. Conrad's claim to the throne was recognized only in Italy thanks to papal support, and it was there that he imprisoned Meginher. Shortly before the Italian expedition of 1136, Conrad and Lothar made peace. Conrad was subsequently elected and reigned as King Conrad III (r. 1138–1152).

Conrad elevated to the kingship. Indeed, Albero brought it about through hard work that Duke Frederick (King Conrad's brother) and Bishop Burchard of Worms met with Conrad himself at a gathering in Coblenz.[53] At that meeting, Archbishop Arnulf of Cologne appeared, and finally after much consultation lord Archbishop Albero elevated Conrad to the kingship. And conducting him with a great multitude to Aachen, Albero confirmed Conrad in the kingdom by anointing him king.[54]

Afterwards, the Saxons (along with Duke Henry, King Lothar's son-in-law) appointed a day and place at Hersfeld for King Conrad, so that they might decide through trial by combat whether or not Conrad might rightfully begin to rule.[55] And although Archbishop Albero had promised that he would come with twenty knights, he led 500 knights and brought with him thirty cart-loads of wine and an immense amount of provisions and, by all estimates, an almost infinite number of wagons. There Albert the younger, then Archbishop of Mainz, was trying hard to escalate the incident into a full-scale conflict. Lord Albero, on the other hand, with the help of God, took care that the armies were peacefully kept apart from one another, although many thousands had come together in great anger to fight. Once having reconciled everyone in peace, Archbishop Albero sent a cart-load of wine to each prince, particularly to the Saxon magnates. The subtlety

53. Frederick II von Staufen was Duke of Swabia from 1105–1147, and Burchard or Bucco II was bishop of Worms from 1120–1149. The election took place on 7 March 1138.

54. The person who in fact consecrated Conrad on 13 March was the papal legate Dietwin, assisted by Albero and the Archbishop-elect Arnold von Berg of Cologne (r. 1137–1151), to whom the prerogative to consecrate pertained since Aachen lay in his see.

55. Henry the Proud (d. 1139), duke of both Saxony and Bavaria, was Lothar's designated heir and the holder of the imperial insignia. But many nobles feared that Henry would be too powerful a monarch, and so they accepted Conrad's election. The confrontation at Hersfeld in Saxony took place in July or August 1139. Albert or Adelbert II von Saarbrücken was archbishop of Mainz from 1138–1141.

of lord Albero's ingenuity in this matter should be noted: he reasoned that a supply of wine and other provisions works for victory and inspires men's minds more than many thousands of starving soldiers.

[Origins of the War over St. Maximin, 1139]
21. When these things had been accomplished, Albero accepted the abbey of Saint Maximin from King Conrad for this and other services.[56] Indeed the king restored to him the patronage of the abbey, which had been a royal possession for a long time. When this became known through the winged breath of rumor, the monks, who had been living exceedingly well in the abbey, gathered together all their precious stones and gems, as well as silver and gold, which in those days were plentiful in that monastery both in woven tapestries, various pictures and furniture. And before the archbishop's return, the monks gave it all to the Count of Namur (who at that time held the land of Luxemburg),[57] so that the count with his military forces would bring armed help to them and, because he was the advocate of their abbey, remove from them the archbishop's dominion and power.

Now this narrative needs courage; now the material presented to us is insurmountable and requires not my weak pen, but some sort of great poet. Who would be able to match in mere words the heroic acts of this worthy man Albero and his men against the aforesaid tyrant, who contended for seven years with guile, sword, fire, famine and the inexplicable reversals in the fortunes of war? This subject

56. The privilege was issued in May 1139.
57. Count Henry IV of Luxemburg (r. 1136–1196), later known as "the Blind," sought to use his advocacy over St. Maximin to expand his own rule in the region. The country of Luxemburg would be established by his successors. Balderich and his contemporaries preferred to name Count Henry after his possession of Namur, now part of Belgium.

would be worthy of the skills of Homer, if indeed he were worthy of the subject. If I were to wish to render in poetry the glorious acts of each individual man, the various outcomes of war in martial combat and the diverse fortunes of now one side then the other retreating and advancing, or if, with the expertise of historians, I depicted for you, dear reader, each event brought to life through well-crafted narration as though you saw it happening before your eyes, then either I should succumb to the burden (which is the truth), or else I would be found not unequal to Virgil, Statius, Livy or Josephus.[58] But even if I were sufficient to the task, my flute would not be great enough. For this book would be less than those actions about which it is written. But I do not believe that he, who might have done this work well, should be less praised than all those whose deeds he has individually portrayed. But for now you can expect nothing more from me than that I summarily touch on every event lest they be completely lost in eternal oblivion.

[Albero and Pope Innocent]

22. At the time when the church of Saint Maximin was lacking a pastor, the monks elected as abbot a monk from the church of Liège, a brother of some advisors to the Count of Namur, so that by their counsel the count might be daily more fiercely inflamed into fury.[59] Against the wishes of the archbishop, they led this man to Rome with great extravagance and had him blessed as abbot by lord Pope Innocent. The populace was astonished at such a sudden change of events, namely that the Roman Church so

---

58. Virgil (70–19 BC) is best known as the author of the *Aeneid,* an epic poem about the fall of Troy and the origins of Rome. The poet Statius (AD 45–96) was known in the Middle Ages for his *Thebaïd,* an epic about the wars between the sons of Oedipus. Titus Livius or Livy (ca. 59 BC–AD 17) wrote a massive history of Rome from its beginnings (*Ab urbe condita*), and Josephus (ca. AD 38–ca. 100) wrote histories of the Jews and their wars with the Romans (*Bellum Iudaicum*).

59. Siger was Abbot of St. Maximin from 1139 to at least 1163.

gravely mistreated such a great and worthy man as Albero, who had borne so many labors and so many dangers on the church's behalf, who not so long ago had been in such grace with the apostolic see, and who on behalf of Pope Innocent had so set himself against King Lothar during the Italian expedition that the archbishop and the king had departed from one another in discord.

[Albero's Success, 1140]

23. Likewise, at the time of this war between the archbishop and the count, the brothers of the church of Coblenz also began to trouble Albero.[60] For against Albero's wishes they elected the nobleman lord Ludwig von Isenburg as provost; and journeying with Ludwig to Rome at great expense, they brought back to the lord archbishop apostolic letters contradicting his wishes.[61] When the brothers presented these letters to the archbishop while he was presiding over a synod, he threw the letters to the ground in anger. For that reason he was called to account before lord Pope Innocent and was summoned by the pope on the appointed day. And when Albero did not come on that day, he was suspended from episcopal office.

All these misfortunes came upon him at the same time, and the Lord freed him from them all. Travelling to Rome, Albero brought it about that the abbot of Saint Maximin both promised obedience and by an oath swore fidelity to him. And he also annulled the election made by those of Coblenz. These events having been resolved, let us return to the count.[62]

60. The foundation of St. Florin in Coblenz. Albero wanted to preserve his right to approve the provost there.

61. These letters were issued on 8 May 1140.

62. Albero had reconciled with Innocent and confirmed his privileges by December 1140.

[The War over St. Maximin]

24. At beginning of this conflict, without warning and before he had broken his oath to Albero his lord, the count approached the city of Trier with 1500 knights. Furthermore, Trier was not fortified. Neither ditches nor walls surrounded it, for, having long existed in peace, the city was unaccustomed to war. And the archbishop himself was absent, attending the royal court.[63] The count might have been able to inflict great damage on the city at the time, if God had not averted this evil. Fortunately, Count Frederick von Vianden[64] was then in the city and, meeting with the Count of Namur, through much persuasion made him turn back. He pointed out that Namur would be held in great and perpetual infamy were he to commit such an act against his lord before he had renounced Albero's lordship. In particular, it would be an offense against the king's majesty if the Count of Namur inflicted this sort of evil while the archbishop was at the court by royal mandate. Upon returning from the court, however, the archbishop began to work to keep the peace and to recall the count from the madness he had undertaken. The count, nonetheless, burned, plundered and slaughtered throughout the bishopric. At last, the archbishop began to defend himself. And since now I hasten to the end, skimming over much, I will summarize the principal deeds.

[The Conflict with the Count of Luxemburg]

25. Albero twice surrounded the castle of Mount Rudolf, which seemed in all ways unconquerable, and destroyed it on the second siege.[65] He built a new castle, called Mount

63. The court may have been in early February 1140 in Worms or in late April in Frankfurt.

64. Count Frederick von Vianden (r. 1124-1152) was one of the local nobles working with (here) and against (Chapter 26) the dominion of the Archbishop of Trier.

65. The location of this castle is unknown, but it was probably on the lower Saar.

Mercury, out of fear that the forces of Namur might occupy that mountain, which was located in the heart of his territory.[66] He captured castle Manderscheid, extremely well-fortified by nature of its location, and retained it up to his death. He took Gerland and Zolver and either captured or destroyed thirty other fortifications of the Count of Namur.[67] He also captured Echternach, in which the count was accustomed to maintain an army.

And between the first and second siege of Mount Rudolf the archbishop and the count met openly on the field of battle. This is how it happened. When the archbishop first besieged Mount Rudolf, the count attacked Pfalzel and, setting fire to the Church of St. Mary, he hoped to burn the archbishop's fortification as well. When that news reached the archbishop, he abandoned the siege and hastened with his army through an entire night so that he might make a show of his strength by attacking the enemy unprepared and striking with an unexpected terror. In fact, the count learned in advance through his scouts of the archbishop's approach, turned in flight, and retreated that night to the episcopal village of Wittlich. There he wished refresh his men and horses, but finding nothing there, he burned the whole village. Proceeding from there to a place near the abbey of Himmerod, the Count of Namur wished to pause and break bread, for he was famished, but it was announced that the army of the archbishop was already almost upon him. While the count swiftly prepared to take flight with his men, he had one of the brothers called to him, and enjoined through a sworn promise that the brother would repeat these words to the archbishop, who was pursuing him: "May God grant you no better day or night than the two days and two nights I have just had. For two days I have had nothing to eat, and on the third I was not even allowed to take a little bread."

66. The castle Neuerburg above Wittlich.
67. The location of Gerland is unknown. Zolver may have been on a hill near the city of Luxembourg.

And so the archbishop overtook the count and engaged in a fierce battle with him. The count, turning tail, scarcely managed to flee with the aid of a swift horse, while most of his men were captured and many indeed were killed. And returning from there to Mount Rudolf, as was said above, the archbishop destroyed it.

Finally the count ran out of strength, and at Speyer through King Conrad (who was then about to go on the crusade to Jerusalem) with great labor and many attempts he sought the grace of the archbishop and with great difficulty gained it.[68] The count confirmed under oath that he would never again take up arms against the Trier church on behalf of Saint Maximin nor would he rebuild Mount Rudolf nor permit it to be rebuilt, and would never retake Manderscheid either by force or extortion. Echternach and the count's other castles and fortifications the archbishop returned to him. And of the great number of benefices the count had held in tenure from the church of Trier, the archbishop returned those he had not already given to his own retainers during the time of this conflict. And thus Albero obtained the Abbey of Saint Maximin and a glorious victory over the Count of Namur. He also accomplished many other things after this.

[Castle Arras and Count Frederick]
26. For although the archbishop had installed Count Frederick von Vianden as warden of one tower in his castle Arras, Frederick usurped the whole castle and pillaged the Mosel River valley. After taking the castle back again, Albero expelled Count Frederick. Much impoverished after all these events because of the great and varied expenses which he had run up during the war, Albero had peace thereafter because after this no one attempted to challenge him in war. And gathering great wealth again, he filled his palace and all his castles with much wine and all kinds of

---

68. The treaty was agreed to in January 1147.

provisions so that he would not find himself unprepared if anyone provoked him again with some injury.

[Albero and Pope Eugene in France, 1147]
27. In those days it happened that the lord Pope Eugene came to France. Albero hurried to meet him at Provins and celebrated Easter with him in Paris.[69] And there he confirmed the privileges of his church by renewing those concerning the primacy of his church and the abbey of Saint Maximin. And he was greatly honored there with appropriate gifts from the lord pope, from King Louis of France and from Count Thibaut.[70] And as he was about to return from there, Albero invited the lord pope to his home.

Albero also brought back to Trier with him from Paris a certain cleric by the name of Balderich, a young man who came from the castle Florennes in the bishopric of Liège. Albero had heard him in the papal court, arguing cases and often pleading suitably. And he made Balderich the schoolmaster in the cathedral of St. Peter, and as long as he lived, held him very close and dear.

Not long afterwards, the aforementioned King of France and Henry, the son of Count Thibaut, travelled through the village of Saint Arnual. When the archbishop learned about it, he sent to each of them such a grand and magnificent amount of provisions that they were exceedingly amazed when it was unexpectedly offered to them.[71]

69. Pope Eugene III (r. 1145–1153) was in Provins on 13 April 1147; Easter that year was on 20 April.

70. King Louis VII ruled from 1137 to 1180. Count Thibaut II (the Great) was born ca. 1090, became count of Chartres, Blois and Brie in 1102, and of Champagne in 1125; he died in 1152.

71. Count Henry I (the Generous) of Champagne and Brie was born in 1127 and reigned from 1152 to 1181. His wife, Marie de Champagne, the daughter of King Louis VII and Eleanor of Aquitaine, was a great patron of the arts.

[Pope Eugene in Trier, 1147–1148]

28. In the same year, on the Sunday when "Ad te levavi" is sung, the lord Pope Eugene came to Trier, just as he had been invited by the lord archbishop to do, and on the Sabbath before that Sunday was honorably received in the church of Saint Eucharius.[72] On that same Sunday he was ushered into the cathedral with the utmost respect by the clergy and people, with an unusually splendid procession and a memorable solemnity. Leading the pope on the right was lord Albero and on the left, Archbishop Arnulf of Cologne, and preceding them were many bishops of Germany, Belgica, France, England, Burgundy, Lombardy, Tuscany and every nation which is under heaven.[73]

Neither am I loath to list the cardinals who came to Trier with lord pope Eugene. These men were indeed honorable in countenance, attire, bearing, knowledge and conduct, and for their great integrity they are worthy of immortal memory. These are their names, and may they have been written better in the book of life: cardinal bishops Alberich of Ostia, Himerus of Tusculum; cardinal priests Guido Summanus, Haribert of Saint Anastasia, master Guidodens (a highly literate man and expert in the law), Julius of Saint Marcello, Hugo of Novara, master Hubald, Giselbert of Saint Mark, John Papiro; from the cardinal deacons Octavian (a man of noble birth, and even more noble in conduct, who should be noted for his integrity and liberality and his special affection for Ger-

---

72. *Ad te levavi* is the introit sung on the first Sunday of Advent, which would have been on 30 November 1147. Pope Eugene III, in a rare papal visit, stayed until February 1148. Eugene also dedicated the new choir of St. Eucharius, now known as St. Matthew, which lay just to the south of medieval Trier.

73. The term Belgica is retained since it refers to the Roman geographical territory. Belgica is not modern Belgium, but the region from just east of the Seine to the mouth of the Scheldt river, stretching southeast in a broad arc to just west of the Rhine near Coblenz, then south to the source of the Mosel. Note also its use in Albero's attempt to assert his primacy in Chapter 29 below and in the memorial verses at the end.

mans), Guido of Cremona (a man of noble blood, very courteous and honorable, and delightfully eloquent), Odo Bonacasa (a most gentle man, from the Roman nobility, who is affable and pious in all things), also John of Saint Maria Nova (a man of the most agreeable affability, who is adorned with holiness of character), also Gregory of Saint Angelo (a man of swift wit, who is prepared and ready for anything which pertains to the integrity and the utility of God's church).[74] What shall I say about Hyacinth? He surpasses every hyacinth flower in the splendor of his virtue, who through the sweetness of his eloquence draws everyone into his love; to see and to hear him was to become acquainted with integrity. Neither will I omit Guido of Pisa, a most prudent man, and notable for his brevity of speech. For twelve weeks without interruption the archbishop took care of all their needs in such abundance that they even declared Plenty had come to them with her horn full.

What shall I record concerning the arrival of archbishops, bishops, abbots, archdeacons, provosts, dukes and counts coming to the lord pope in Trier, not even one of whom departed lacking the archbishop's largesse? Who can set down in words the solemnity of Christmas celebrated in Trier at that time so that you, who did not see it, might be able to understand or imagine it? You may believe it was a brilliant procession on that holy day, when the lord pope, riding upon a horse covered with a richly draped horsecloth, with a multitude of cardinals and bishops on horses covered in white going before him, proceeded to the Church of Saint Paulin.[75] And then returning to the church of St. Peter, he performed the solemnities of the Masses before

74. Balderich likely knew many of these men personally from his time at the papal court. The notable cardinals are: Octavian, who became the anti-pope Victor IV (r. 1159–1164); Guido of Cremona who became the anti-pope Paschal III (r. 1164–1168); and Hyacinth, who became Pope Celestine III (r. 1191–1198).

75. The collegial foundation of St. Paulin lay just outside medieval Trier's gates, beyond St. Maximin.

such a great crowd of people that you could not find a free space more than a foot wide in the whole church. Or what can I say about how on that holy day, after the Divine Office was finished, adorned with the symbols of their offices, they sat down across from each other to eat at the banquet, on one side the lord pope with his cardinals and on the opposite side the lord archbishop with those bishops who had come there? By what art could anyone add up so great and so many expenses? I might add further that, before the arrival of the lord pope, the archbishop built within six weeks a three-storey house which is called "The Pope's." And he also repaired the house called "Jerusalem," which had been nearly in ruins. But even if I were silent, the events will speak for themselves and be recalled to memory.

[Church Council at Rheims, 1148]

29. Now I move on to when Pope Eugene left Trier and went to Rheims to preside over a council during the middle of Lent.[76] Archbishop Albero came to that council in such magnificence that all eyes opened wide and mouths gaped at him. He was borne between two horses in a sedan chair made of leather, befittingly covered on the inside with linen cloth, which was marvelous for all to behold. Albero was already afflicted with old age, and he was failing, broken by his long labors.

Accordingly, at this council he was seated first in order among all bishops, and he had many privileges concerning the primacy of his see over all Belgica, Gaul, and Germany read aloud.[77] Upon hearing these, the Archbishop of Rheims was not a little disturbed. As a result, his men started a fight with Albero's men, and some of them were injured. The lord archbishop Albero reacted very angrily to this and threatened to besiege Ivois and lay waste to the bishopric

76. The council convened in late March 1148.
77. Like Belgica, Gaul is retained here because it refers to the ancient Roman province which extended from the Loire to the Rhine.

of Rheims.[78] And the matter was finally concluded thus:
the Archbishop of Rheims with the Bishop of Soissons came
to Albero's lodging and delivered into his power the men
who had committed the offense.[79]

[Castle Treis and the Count Palatine, 1148]
30. In the month of September of that same year, although
the Palatine Count Herman had occupied castle Treis and
strengthened it with fortifications, Otto Count von Rheineck gave the aforesaid castle and its attendant lands to the
archbishop and his church, so that Otto might get the
castle back.[80] Therefore, Albero besieged castle Treis. The
Count Palatine, however, gathering all his troops, came to
liberate the castle; and he pitched camp at the entrance to
the woods where the castle lay.

On the opposite side, the archbishop drew up a battle
line of soldiers on horse and on foot and for three days
awaited the count's advance. There you would have seen
glittering helmets, coats of mail surpassing the day in splendor, shields lighting up the surrounding hills in the gleaming
sun. What intrepid countenances you would have beheld!
How impatiently the men bore the wait for the slow-to-
arrive enemy. What military exercises by soldiers simulating
combat in arms you would have seen! You would have seen
a fierce horse whirled around in a small space. You would
have witnessed clashes of mounted knights, and lances
splintering with loud cracks. What shouting, both of those
pursuing and of those fleeing, you would have heard! You
would have observed by what art flight is feigned, and then

78. Samson was archbishop of Rheims from 1140 to 1161. Ivois lay
to the northeast of Rheims, within the Empire.
79. Jocelin was bishop of Soissons from 1126 to 1152.
80. King Conrad III had appointed Herman von Stahleck (d. 1156) as
Count Palatine by the Rhine in 1142, ignoring Otto von Rheineck's claims.
Herman's aggressive pursuit of the Palatinate's lands and rights had
stripped Otto of most of his possessions. Otto's attempt to hold onto Treis
by reasserting his vassal status under Albero indicates his weak position.

how those fleeing suddenly turned about, and, their fortune reversed, with a headlong charge they compelled those who were just now pursuing to take flight. There you would have noted that the knights charged first close together, then opened themselves up and ingeniously, as if yielding, received the attacking enemy into the gap, and then surrounded the enemy as the wings of the army came back together. There a thousand arts, a thousand ways of deceiving, were presented for instruction.

Meanwhile, a scout of the archbishop, who had examined the forces of the Count Palatine, arrived and announced that the count was already advancing, prepared for battle. Then you would have seen old Albero himself, although enfeebled in body, personally draw up the battle line of foot soldiers and position his horsemen with military art. Those he knew he addressed one by one by name, and those there whom he did not know he inquired who they might be so that from this inquiry they felt they had gained not merely the acknowledgement of so great a prince, but also his friendship.

Then, holding the archiepiscopal cross in his hands, he began to make an exhortatory oration to the ranks of his soldiers in such a manner: "Oh you friends of the blessed Peter! Oh defenders of the Holy Church, who today for God and for justice have set your mortal bodies against the enemy's sword. Now may the blessed Peter come to you in spirit, for you are his knights today. Believe that he with a great heavenly host protects you today by their invisible shields. Be certain of victory. Behold this sign of the cross, this sign, I say, terrible for the adversaries of Jesus Christ. This is the cross upon which Herman, Count Palatine, swore fidelity to me on that day when I made him an advocate of our Church, on that day when I conferred on him those powers and that authority by which he now attacks me. I told him then that in this cross is a piece of the Lord's cross, upon which He, whose sacrosanct image shines here, triumphed over the enemy of the human race; and I pointed out that the relics of many other venerable saints were contained in this cross. Indeed, that same Count Palatine, holding his hand upon this holy image, swore to me with these words: 'I give to you, lord archbishop, this Lord, He who was crucified for us, as my guarantor, and I swear to you by His virtue that I shall never do anything against you, and that I shall assist you faithfully in all your interests with all my military forces and with all my strength.' Let everyone know that this guarantor, namely Lord Christ, I shall now bring before the count in this his sacred image. I shall thrust it before his eyes; I shall show this witness of his oath to him.

"But now, oh faithful of Jesus Christ, who offer your life and blood for the defense of His church, prepare your heart for the Lord, cleanse your consciences. And because there is no time for you to make individual confessions, make to me, your pastor, a general confession of your sins; and by the power given to me by God through my office, I shall make indulgence and remission for you of all your sins so that if today anyone should be called from this temporal and uncertain life, he may cross over to a better one, namely eternal life."

Then when he had accepted the public confession of everyone and granted forgiveness and absolution by making a blessing upon them, he so inspired them all that no sign of fearfulness appeared in anyone. The archbishop himself entrusted his banner to the Count of Namur, while he carried the cross in his own hands. While these things were taking place, the Palatine Count discovered through his scouts that he was no match to fight a battle against such inspired troops. He sent legates to the archbishop and charged them to say supplicatory words; and so that I may quickly come to the end, he brought it about that those of his men who were in the castle might leave unharmed. And so the archbishop fulfilled his desire concerning castle Treis.

[Albero's Character]

31. And now it pleases me to relate a few things concerning Albero's character and customs. Indeed, he had strange and exceedingly unusual habits in everything he did. He was slow in body and action and speech. He drew everything out for an extremely long time; never, or very rarely, did he do something in haste. He contrived such a delay in everything that he seemed ponderous and dithering, and he made both his own people and strangers exhausted. Although any project which he began seemed hopeless because of his excessive procrastination, nevertheless it was always completed according to the desired end.

Neither in walking, nor in riding, nor in sleeping, nor in waking did he hold to the fashion of other men. In walking he was led by the hands, for he had sciatica. And on account of this infirmity, when he rode, he had the stirrups hanging over the saddlebow and placed his left leg over the neck of the horse. Although he did this because he was forced to by his illness, it seemed to others he did it to show off. At night he was accustomed to be in counsel or conference all the way to the early hours or cockcrow, often even up to daybreak, and he most often slept until the second hour of the day. He came late to his table after the usual hour and lingered for a very long time at the table, disputing and conferring most happily with his clerics about sacred scriptures and the opinions of the holy fathers, for he was accustomed to surround himself with a great crowd of religious and literate men.

In the holy mysteries of the altar Albero seemed more than human. He never approached them without tears and the utmost contrition. When attired in his pontifical robes, he seemed an angel of God, for he shone with an angelic countenance. He performed those celestial sacraments with such devotion that while engaged in these liturgical secrets he seemed through contemplation and prayer to gain entrance to heaven. When he preached a sermon to the people, he could hardly make clear those things which he chose: first because he was slow in speech; second because being born in French-speaking territory he was not fluent in German; last because the mysteries he dealt with were too profound. Almost everything he said was in proverbs and parables; he possessed a greater quantity of them than any other man to our knowledge. He distributed alms daily and in as great a quantity as possible. And he was exceedingly skilled in physiognomy, to such a degree that he would discern the secrets of character and behavior from different facial appearances.

When Albero went to the royal court he was a sight for all to behold. He alone seemed worthy of admiration; by the magnificence of his entourage and disbursement he put all the other princes in the shade. By his pleasant speech and his very amusing interjection of proverbs, he was accustomed to charm both king and princes. He used to come to the court or whatever meeting last and long awaited, and he was always the last to leave. Never in an assembly did he offer his counsel without first hearing others out.

[The Trip to and from the Royal Court at Frankfurt, 1149]
32. I, Balderich, who have written this small book, was present at one court that Albero attended at Frankfurt under King Conrad.[81] Albero travelled there with forty transport ships, not counting the swift warships, cargo vessels and cooking galleys. At that court he had with him eight counts, Duke Matthew of Lotharingia, Duke Henry of Limburg, and such a multitude of clerics and knights that everyone who saw them expressed admiration.[82] He also brought with him on his own ship Master Gerland of Besançon and Master Thierry of Chartres, the two most distinguished doctors in fame and renown in our time, and

81. This court took place in mid-August 1149.
82. Duke Matthew of Lotharingia (r. 1139–1176); Duke Henry of Limburg (r. 1139–1167) ruled a territory to the north of Trier.

he greatly delighted in their disputation and discussion.[83] Upon returning from the court, he sent them home happy and generously honored with appropriate gifts.

I do not know, however, whether this is worth remembering, but, since he held only disdain and perhaps suspicion towards the people of Mainz, when he was returning from the aforesaid court and approaching their city, he ordered the war flags hoisted on all the ships and his knights to show themselves in their glittering golden shields, mail, and helmets, surpassing the gleam of silver. Approaching with horns and trumpets, the clash of weapons, and the horrible-sounding war-song of the men, he upset the whole city. There you could have seen men assembling from all over town, women crying out, and tumult and terror everywhere, as if the city was about to be captured.

[Albero's Last Days and Last Words, 1152]
Now that I am about to end this narration, I shall say a few things about his last days, his death and his testament.

33. He held a great court at Coblenz during the Lord's Epiphany and concluded a truce between the Count of Molbach and the Count of Sayn.[84] For a long time these men had waged war with each other over the county of Bonn, and in this war the nobles of almost every lowland region had become involved. And they would have devastated the whole land if Albero had not intervened with his council. For it was his custom frequently to assemble his suffragans and the princes and nobles from his province to administer the incomes generously and to manage those incomes with

83. Gerland or Jarland of Besançon was a theologian. Thierry or Theodore of Chartres (d. ca. 1150 in Frankfurt) was an important master of the school of philosophy at Chartres.

84. The Count of Bonn had died in 1145 without heirs, triggering the war. This court took place on 6 January 1152. The area around Bonn lay just to the north of Trier's possessions. Molbach, located between Aachen and Cologne, is now known as Untermaubach. Sayn lay just north of Coblenz, within the diocese of Trier, but inside the Archbishop of Cologne's sphere of political influence.

them on behalf of the welfare of the Church and the peace of the fatherland.

And now, as I had begun to say, right after Epiphany, burning with the terrible heat of an acute fever, wracked by the pain of pleurisy, and beginning to doubt his survival, he called together religious men like Abbot Richard of Saint Mary of Springiersbach, Abbot Bertolf of Saint Eucharius, and many others.[85] And making confession of all his sins, he was anointed with oil, according to the instruction of the blessed James.[86] And as he was about to partake in the most holy body of Christ, he said these words, indicative of his great faithfulness and true, catholic faith:

"Listen, my most dear brethren. I have called you abbots and religious men together so that you might stand witness for me concerning my true faith both in the present church and in the universal one in which holy angels and men will come together at the end of the world and that you may assist through your prayers this faith to save me. This, which I now behold in the form of bread, I believe is the true body of Christ the Son of God, which was then, and remains now, united with the word of God, the true Son of the most high Father, in the virginal womb of Mary the unstained virgin, overshadowed by the Holy Ghost, and that for our sake, it was briefly separated from His soul in death on the cross. While His soul descended to hell, his body in the tomb was not deprived of the divine fellowship; neither was His soul left in hell. David testified to this, saying: 'For thou dost not give me up to hell; or let thy godly one see the Pit.'[87] This, I say, is that body of Christ, which revived on the third day (the spirit having returned to it), and having broken the gates of hell through divine virtue and snatched from the power of the devil the faithful of earlier

85. Springiersbach was a notable Cistercian foundation in the Eifel supported by Albero.
86. James 5:14–15.
87. Ps 16:10.

times, rose from the tomb, beyond death or pain thereafter. And at the meal before His passion, holding Himself in His own sacred hands, He shared with His disciples this body to be eaten in the form of bread, giving them a body which could not suffer pain, although He was just about to suffer it, and teaching them to celebrate the mysteries of this sacrament. This, I say, is the body of Christ, which, by the power of His will (by which He did everything He willed to do), appeared to the disciples visible and tangible and yet incorruptible for forty days after the resurrection. This is the truly glorified and ineffably glorious body, which was miraculously assumed into glory while the apostles looked on, and sits as Lord with the Lord, the Son at the right hand of the Father, in the bosom of the Father, namely in a unity of being. This sacred and venerable body, I can truly say with the centurion, I am not worthy to have come under my roof.[88]

"I ask, however, oh good Jesus, You who deigned to enter the house of Zacchaeus, that You may deign also to come into the innermost and secret dwelling of my soul, and cleanse my soul, because I have sinned against You.[89] And You, who have already come to me through this faith, visit me with indwelling grace. And in this faith I receive life for the sake of life, just as You have said: 'The bread which I shall give for the life of the world is my flesh.'[90] May it be for me a clear road toward eternal life. Amen."

And when he had partaken of the body of the Lord, he took the chalice and said: "Oh most holy and serene Father, today I, a sinner, beseech Your most benign Majesty that through this true sacrifice of the body and blood of our lord Jesus Christ, through this inestimable mystery of human redemption and eternal salvation, which Your holy church

88. Cf. Matt 8:8.
89. Zacchaeus was a publican or tax-gatherer, at whose house Jesus stayed on the way to Jerusalem (Luke 19:2–10).
90. John 6:51.

offers You, in true faith, in pious propitiation, and in the blood of Your son, may You be gentle and well-disposed toward me. And since, according to the sacred gift of Your teaching, I believe this to be the true body of Your son, spare me today and take away my iniquity; and do not condemn me, but by the truth of this faith, lead me on the righteous path to eternal life. Amen."

[Albero's Will and Funeral]
34. Know, dear reader, that if these were not Albero's very words, I have rendered nonetheless his thoughts and the meaning of his words. Now I will explain, as briefly as I can what sort of will he drew up. The manor of Thüre, which he bought with money from Count William of Gleiberg, he gave to the brothers of the Church of St. Peter in Trier, so that on the anniversary of his death they might have a meal there.[91] And he donated his paternal estate at Säul, and the manor Briedel,[92] to the aforesaid church with the stipulation that from its incomes the gilt cross, whose gilding had been stripped off at the time of the aforesaid war, should be repaired, and that certain ornaments, which had been pawned, should be restored. And finally he ceded the manor perpetually to the use of the brothers.

He died on the fifteenth of January.[93] And although he succumbed to the common fate of mortals, nonetheless he was not buried according to the common fortune of men. For although he died at Coblenz, but his intestines were interred at Himmerod, against the wall which faces north and under a marble stone, while his body, preserved with myrrh, aloe and aromatics by his most skillful physician Philip Lombard (who had predicted his death three days

91. The counts of Gleiberg were related to the Luxemburgers, and based on the Lahn River. Thüre was near Mayen.
92. Säul is in Luxemburg; Briedel is on the middle Mosel.
93. He, in fact, died on 18 January 1152, as correctly stated below.

before by inspecting his urine),[94] and adorned in episcopal vestments was then borne to Trier with a great escort. Count Palatine Herman and many barons of the lowland region followed his funeral procession with a great retinue.

Finally, when he had come to Trier, the clergy and people advanced to meet him at the Mosel bridge, and each day with a densely attended procession he was borne through a different monastery, one day for each monastery. And each day more and more great men from throughout the province flowed in to attend his funeral. Learning of his death, his suffragan bishops, Stephan of Metz, Henry of Toul, Albero of Verdun came,[95] as did Jordan, cardinal priest of the Roman church, who at that time had convened in Metz an assembly in Metz of all the abbots of Upper Lotharingia, and the latter came with him to Albero's funeral.[96] And with such honor and communal mourning by the whole province, Albero was buried on the eleventh day after his death. Everyone who had come confessed that they had never seen so estimable a funeral. Albero's sepulchre is in the cathedral of blessed Peter, on the south side next to the altar of blessed Stephan. And it should be noted that while he was still alive, every time he entered the cathedral he was accustomed to pray in the selfsame place where he now has his sepulchre.

[Prayer for Albero and Memorial Poem]
35. Lord Jesus Christ, splendor and wisdom and virtue of the Father, who in Your ineffable worthiness shone in human form so that You might liberate us miserable sinners from the power of the devil through the fellowship of Your intimate association with us, may the light of Your brilliance shine today on Albero, a priest of the true sacri-

94. Nothing more is known about this physician.
95. Bishop Albero of Verdun reigned from to 1131 1156.
96. Cardinal Jordan, who served from 1145 to 1154, was also the chamberlain for Pope Eugene III.

fice, according to the order of Melchizedek, who frequently in holy faith offered to Your Father Your sacrosanct and venerable body, which You gave to Your church as a pledge of Your love, when Your Father requested. For when Your Father spoke in the synagogue: "Will I drink the blood of goats or bulls?"[97] David heard this and, like a devoted servant alluding to Your Father, answered speaking of your gracious purpose: "Burnt sacrifice and sin offering Thou dost not desire."[98] And when Your Father seemed to agree, foreshadowing His will and Yours, he said in your persona, or rather You said in his: "Lo, I come."[99] And Your church repudiated the old rite of sacrifice (since it saw that the flesh of bulls and goats which the synagogue offered to You did not please you), and anxious about what it might offer to You in praise and acknowledgement for all Your gifts, the Church asked every day: "What shall I render to the Lord for all his bounty to me?"[100] Then, with miraculous compassion You put on Your body, and gave it to Your spouse, Your friend, Your dove, namely Your Church so that it might sacrifice it to Your Father. For which reason the Church joyously says: "I will lift up the cup of salvation, and call on the name of the Lord."[101] Therefore, in virtue of this sacrifice deign to give the brilliance of Your countenance and eternal rest to Albero, Lord, who lives and reigns as God through all ages. Amen.

Albero, you pre-eminent man, Rome weeps, in every quarter weeps Trier,
You who have died were so great, so amazing a man.
Rome mourns the passing of Trier's upright pastor,

97. Cf. Ps 50:13. Melchizedek is mentioned in Gen 14:18 as both King of Salem and a priest of God. For theologians and political theorists of the Middle Ages, Melchizedek typified rulers who wielded spiritual and temporal power, such as popes and prince-bishops.
98. Ps 40:6. See also Hebr 10:4–7.
99. Ps 40:7.
100. Ps 116:12.
101. Ps 116:13.

Orderer of justice, light of the church.
You were great to the great, simple to the simple-folk, a bane
　　to tyrants,
A model for the rich, a sharer with the poor.
The castles of tyrants you razed, while many good castles
You raised; generous and hospitable you were,
Generous and humane; Janus had completed in sequence
Eight and ten days; may death be a rest for you.

[Epitaphs]
36. These ten verses, written in gold letters on a copper
plate, are preserved as Archbishop Albero of Trier's epitaph.
Below the arch:

Belgica Roma, your honor and your perpetual glory,[102]
Here he lies, who for you lives in everlasting honor.
Albero, light of the world, honor of the city, glory of the
　　clergy,
Renowned of the fatherland, and splendor of the church,
A small part of him rests here, the greater still lives,
For his spirit lives on, his fame will be never ceasing.
Oh, such a great man enclosed within such a pitiful tomb.
Not less than worldwide has been his praise and esteem.
It was his special lot not to be conquered, but to conquer; to
　　the conquered
He was merciful; in generosity he had no equal.
Here the man, here he is, to whom primates bent their necks.
Belgica Germania has had none greater.
Kind Trier, made greater through his man, to you
Rome sent Quirites; he made them citizens and your own.[103]
And hither came the leader of the world; here is the heart of
　　the world —

102. Belgica Roma and Belgica Germania eleven lines later refer
again to the Roman provinces.
103. *Quirites* was a legal term used for the citizens of ancient Rome.
The use of the term here is unclear.

He does not deny this, and your name is "the Second Rome."[104]
Janus twice nine times had brought the sun to the world,
When it took away such a light of the church.
What alone remains, speak, reader, with a supplicant spirit:
Albero, may light shine upon you, may life in God be yours.
He, who, as if from a watchtower, able to view the whole world,
Has carried your name, Trier, up to the stars.
Confounding the mighty, and an iron rod to the proud,
He knew how to break them like a potter's vessel.[105]
No misfortune was able to render him less,
He was greater when hard-pressed.
He, a house of God, a mountain higher than mountains,
    towering
High over the hills casting shadows over his valleys.
And when Janus had called the sun to rise twice nine times
An unclouded star has fallen at its setting.
"Death," said Albero, "is nothing to me, since again will rise
The flesh, glorified, celebrating with the soul."

This is the epitaph above his relics in Coblenz:

Prelate venerable for both his office and his worthiness,
Albero has interred here, alas, only his heart and his entrails.
Ask of God, dear reader, that the man, whom you shall like-
    wise follow,
May be found there, where true peace may be for you.

104. This is a reference to Pope Eugene's visit. Trier has a claim to
be second Rome, since according to legend, the Apostle Peter's assistant,
Eucharius, came from Rome to Trier and founded the bishopric.
    105. Ps. 2:9.

Central Europe, ca. 1150

The Mosel Region, ca. 1150

Selected Bibliography

PRIMARY SOURCES

Bernard of Clairvaux. *The Letters of St Bernard of Clairvaux*. Trans. Bruno Scott James. 1953; reprint, Kalamazoo: Cistercian Publications, 1998.

Constitutiones et Acta Publica Imperatorum et Regum. Ed. Ludwig Weiland. *Monumenta Germaniæ Historica, Legum; Sectio 4, Inde ab a. DCCCCXI. usque ad a. MCXCVII*. Hannover: Hahn, 1893.

Gesta Alberonis archiepiscopi auctore Balderico. Ed. G. Waitz. *Monumenta Germaniæ Historica: Scriptores* (in folio) 8:243–60. Hannover: Hahn, 1847. Also available at *Monumenta Germaniae Historica digital* <http://www.dmgh.de/>. Repr. *Patrologiae cursus completus: Series Latina*, ed. J.-P. Migne, 221 vols. (Paris: Migne, 1844–1866), 154: 1307c–1338b. Also available at *Patrologia Latina Database* <http://pld.chadwyck.co.uk/> [subscription required].

Gesta Alberonis metrica auctore anonymo. Ed. G. Waitz. *Monumenta Germaniæ Historica, Scriptores* (in folio) 8:236–43. Hannover: Hahn, 1847.

Vita Theogeri. Ed. Philip Jaffé. *Monumenta Germaniæ Historica, Scriptores* 12:449–79. Hannover: Hahn, 1856.

Wibaldi epistolae. Ed. Philip Jaffé. *Bibliotheca rerum Germanicarum*. 6 vols. *Monumenta Corbeiensia* 1:76–616. Berlin: Weidmann, 1864–1873.

GERMAN TRANSLATIONS OF THE *GESTA ALBERONIS*

Zenz, Emil, ed. and trans. *Von Erzbischof Gottfried (1124) bis zum Tode Alberos (1152): Die Taten der Trierer/ Gesta Treverorum*. Vol. 2. Trier: Paulinus Verlag, 1958.

Kallfelz, Hatto, trans. "Taten Erzbischof Alberos von Trier, verfaßt von Balderich." *Lebensbeschreibungen einiger Bischöfe des 10.–12. Jahrhunderts*, pp. 543–617. Ausgewählte Quellen zur Deutschen Geschichte des Mittelalters, Freiherr vom Stein-Gedächtnisausgabe 22. Darmstadt: Wissenschaftliche Buchgesellschaft, 1973.

SECONDARY SOURCES

Arnold, Benjamin. *Count and Bishop in Medieval Germany: A Study of Regional Power, 1100–1350*. Philadelphia: University of Pennsylvania Press, 1991.

—. *German Knighthood, 1050–1300*. Oxford: Oxford University Press, 1985.

—. *Medieval Germany, 500–1300: A Political Interpretation*. Toronto: University of Toronto Press, 1997.

—. *Princes and Territories in Medieval Germany*. Cambridge: Cambridge University Press, 1991.

Barraclough, Geoffrey. *The Origins of Modern Germany*. 1946; reprint, New York: Capricorn Books, 1963.

—, ed. and trans. *Mediaeval Germany, 911–1250: Essays by German Historians*. 2 vols. Oxford: Basil Blackwell, 1938.

Becker, Adolf. *Die deutschen Handschriften der Stadtbibliothek zu Trier*. Beschreibendes Verzeichnis der Handschriften der Stadtbibliothek zu Trier 7. Trier: Kommissionsverlag der Fr. Lintzschen Buchhandlung, 1911.

Benson, Robert L. *The Bishop-Elect: A Study in Medieval Ecclesiastical Office*. Princeton: Princeton University Press, 1968.

Bernhardi, Wilhelm. *Konrad III. Jahrbücher der Deutschen Geschichte*. 1883; reprint, Berlin: Duncker und Humblot, 1975.

Bliese, John R.E. "Rhetoric and Morale: A Study of Battle Orations from the Central Middle Ages." *Journal of Medieval History* 15 (1989): 201–26.

Blumenthal, Uta-Renate. *The Investiture Controversy: Church and Monarchy from the Ninth to the Twelfth Century*. Philadelphia: University of Pennsylvania Press, 1988.

Bredero, Adriaan H. *Bernard of Clairvaux: Between Cult and History.* Grand Rapids, MI: William B. Eerdmans, 1996.

Büttner, Heinrich. "Der Übergang der Abtei St. Maximin an das Erzstift Trier unter Erzbischof Albero von Montreuil." *Geschichtliche Landeskunde* 5 (1968): 65–77.

Chibnall, Marjorie. *The Empress Mathilda: Queen Consort, Queen Mother and Lady of the English.* Oxford: Blackwell, 1991.

Coué, Stephanie. *Hagiographie im Kontext: Schreibanlass and Funktion von Bischofsviten aus dem 11. and vom Anfang des 12. Jahrhunderts.* Arbeiten zur Frühmittelalterforschung 24. Berlin and New York: de Gruyter, 1997.

Crone, Marie-Louise. *Untersuchungen zur Reichskirchenpolitik Lothars III. (1125–1127) zwischen reichskirchlicher Tradition und Reformkurie.* Frankfurt am Main: Peter Lang, 1982.

Ebenbauer, Alfred. "Das Dilemma der Wahrheit: Gedanken zum historisierenden Roman des 13. Jahrhunderts." In *Geschichtsbewußtsein in der deutschen Literatur des Mittelalters: Tübinger Colloquium 1983*, ed. Christoph Gerhardt, Nigel F. Palmer, and Burghart Wachinger, pp. 52–71. Tübingen: Max Niemeyer Verlag, 1985.

Engels, Odilo. "Der Erzbischof von Trier, der rheinische Pfalzgraf und die gescheiterte Verbandsbildung von Springiersbach im 12. Jahrhundert." In *Secundum Regula Vivere: Festschrift für P. Norbert Backmund, O. Praem.*, ed. Gert Melville, pp. 87–103. Windberg: Poppe-Verlag, 1978.

Erkens, Franz-Reiner. *Die Trierer Kirchenprovinz im Investiturstreit.* Passauer historische Forschungen 4. Cologne and Vienna: Böhlau Verlag, 1987.

Fleckenstein, Josef. "Problematik und Gestalt der ottonisch-salischen Reichskirche." In *Reich und Kirche vor dem Investiturstreit: Vorträge beim wissenschaftlichen Kolloquium aus Anlaß des achtzigsten Geburtstags von*

Gerd Tellenbach, ed. Karl Schmid, pp. 83–98. Sigmaringen: Jan Thorbecke Verlag, 1985.

Fuhrmann, Horst. *Germany in the High Middle Ages, c. 1050–1200*. Trans. Timothy Reuter. Cambridge: Cambridge University Press, 1986.

Freed, John B. *Noble Bondsmen: Ministerial Marriages in the Archdiocese of Salzburg, 1100–1343*. Ithaca: Cornell University Press, 1995.

—. "Reflections on the Medieval German Nobility." *American Historical Review* 91 (1986): 553–75.

Gade, John A. *Luxemburg in the Middle Ages*. Leiden: E. J. Brill, 1951.

Gerstner, Ruth. *Die Geschichte der lothringischen und rheinischen Pfalzgrafschaf von ihrer Anfängen bis zur Ausbildung des Kurterritoriums Pfalz*. Rheinisches Archiv 40. Bonn: Ludwig Röhrscheid Verlag, 1941.

Gleber, Helmut. *Papst Eugen III. (1145–1153) unter besonderer Berücksichtigung seiner politischen Tätigkeit*. Beiträge zur mittelalterlichen und neueren Geschichte 6. Jena: Verlag von Gustav Fischer, 1936.

Haarländer, Stephanie. *Vitae episcoporum: Eine Quellengattung zwischen Hagiographie und Historiographie, untersucht an Lebensbeschreibungen von Bischöfen des Regnum Teutonicum im Zeitalter der Ottonen und Salier*. Monographien zur Geschichte des Mittelalters 47. Stuttgart: Anton Hiersemann, 2000.

Haverkamp, Alfred. *Medieval Germany 1056–1273*. 2nd ed. Oxford: Oxford University Press, 1992.

Housley, Norman. "Crusades Against Christians: Their Origins and Early Development, c. 1000–1216." In *Crusade and Settlement: Papers Read at the First Conference of the Society for the Study of the Crusades and the Latin East and Presented to R.C. Smail*, ed. Peter Edbury, pp. 17–36. Cardiff: University College Cardiff Press, 1985.

Huyskens, Viktor. *Albero von Montreuil: Erzbischof von Trier*, 1. Theil. PhD Dissertation. University of Münster, 1879.

Jaeger, C. Stephen. *The Origins of Courtliness: Civilizing Trends and the Formation of Courtly Ideals 939–1210*. Philadelphia: University of Pennsylvania Press, 1985.

Köhler, Oskar. *Das Bild des geistlichen Fürsten in den Viten des 10., 11. und 12. Jahrhunderts*. Abhandlungen zur mittleren und neuren Geschichte 77. Berlin: Verlag für Staatswissenschaften und Geschichte, GmbH, 1935.

Leyser, Karl. "The German Aristocracy from the Ninth to the Early Twelfth Century: A Historical and Cultural Sketch." In *Medieval Germany and Its Neighbors, 900–1250*, pp. 161–89. London: The Hambledon Press, 1982.

Manitius, Max. *Geschichte der lateinischen Literatur des Mittelalters*. 3 vols. Munich: C.H. Becksche Verlagsbuchhandlung, 1911–31.

Miller, Maureen C. *Power and the Holy in the Age of the Investiture Conflict: A Brief History with Documents*. The Bedford Series in History and Culture. Boston and New York: Bedford/St. Martin's, 2005.

Müller, Jörg R. *Vir religiosus ac strenuus: Albero von Montreuil, Erzbischof von Trier, 1132–1152*. Trierer Historische Forschungen 56. Trier: Kliomedia, 2006.

Panzer, Friedrich. "Erzbischof Albero von Trier und die Deutschen Spielmannsepen." In *Germanistische Abhandlungen, Hermann Paul zum 17. März 1902 dargebracht*, pp. 303–32. Strasbourg: Verlag Karl J. Trübner, 1902.

Parisse, Michel. *Noblesse et chevalerie en Lorraine médiévale: Les familles nobles du XIe au XIIIe siècle*. Nancy: Publications de l'Université de Nancy, 1982.

Pauly, Ferdinand. *Aus der Geschichte des Bistums Trier*. Pt. I: *Von der spätrömischen Zeit bis zum 12. Jahrhundert*. Veröffentlichungen des Bistumsarchiv Trier 13/14. Trier: Selbstverlag des Bistumsarchivs Trier, 1968.

Pavlac, Brian A. "Excommunication and Territorial Politics in High Medieval Trier." *Church History* 60 (1991): 20–36.

Petke, Wolfgang. *Kanzlei, Kapelle und königliche Kurie unter Lothar III. (1125–1137).* Forschungen zur Kaiser- und Papstgeschichte des Mittelalters; Beihefte zu J.F. Böhmer, Regesta Imperii 5. Cologne and Vienna: Böhlau Verlag, 1985.

Prümers, Rodgero. *Albero von Montreuil, Erzbischof von Trier: 1132–1152.* Göttingen: Robert Peppmüller, 1874.

Reuter, Timothy. "The Imperial Church System of the Ottonian and Salian Rulers: A Reconsideration." *Journal of Ecclesiastical History* 33 (1982): 347–74.

Spörl, Johannes. *Grundformen hochmittelalterliche Geschichtsanschauung: Studien zur Weltbild der Geschichtsschreiber des 12. Jahrhunderts.* 1935; reprint, Darmstadt: Wissenschaftliche Buchgesellschaft, 1968.

Tellenbach, Gerd. *Church, State and Christian Society at the Time of the Investiture Contest.* Trans. R.F. Bennett. Oxford: Basil Blackwell, 1966.

Tierney, Brian. *The Crisis of Church and State 1050–1300, with Selected Documents.* Englewood Cliffs, NJ: Prentice-Hall, 1964. Repr. Toronto: University of Toronto Press, 1988.

Wattenbach, Wilhelm and Franz-Josef Schmale. *Deutschlands Geschichtsquellen im Mittelalter: vom Tode Kaiser Heinrichs V. bis zum Ende des Interregnum.* Darmstadt: Wissenschaftliche Buchgesellschaft, 1976.

Weinfurter, Stefan. *The Salian Century: Main Currents in an Age of Transition.* Trans. Barbara M. Bowlus. Philadelphia: University of Pennsylvania Press, 1999.

Werle, Hans. "Die rheinischen Pfalzgrafen als Obervögte des Erzstiftes Trier im 11. und 12. Jahrhundert." *Trierisches Jahrbuch* (1957): 5–14.

Wood, Susan. *The Proprietary Church in the Medieval West.* Oxford: Oxford University Press, 2006.

Ziegler, Wolfram. "Studien zur staufischen Opposition unter Lothar III. (1125–1137)." *Concilium medii aevi* 10 (2007): 67–101.

Zimmer, N. "Albero von Montreuil, Erzbischof von Trier (1132–1152)." *Trierische Chronik: Zeitschrift der Gesellschaft für Trierische Geschichte und Denkmalspflege* 3 (1907):113–23, 145–54.

Index

The index is comprehensive of locations and proper names pertinent to the *Deeds of Albero* of Trier, and includes selected topics covered both in the introduction and text.